THE SHOOTING SCRIPT®

NURSE BETTY

NURSE BETTY

SCREENPLAY BY

JOHN C. RICHARDS &
JAMES FLAMBERG

INTRODUCTION BY

NEIL LaBUTE

A Newmarket Shooting Script® Series Book
NEWMARKET PRESS • NEW YORK

This book is published simultaneously in the United States of America and in Canada.

FIRST EDITION

00 01 02 10 9 8 7 6 5 4 3 2 1

ISBN: 1-55704-455-4

Library of Congress Catalog-in-Publication Data is available upon request.

QUANTITY PURCHASES

Companies, professional groups, clubs, and other organizations may qualify for special terms when ordering quantities of this title. For information, write to Special Sales, Newmarket Press, 18 East 48th Street, New York, NY 10017; call (212) 832-3575 or (800) 669-3903; FAX (212) 832-3629; or Email sales@newmarketpress.com
website www.newmarketpress.com

Manufactured in the United States of America.

OTHER BOOKS IN THE NEWMARKET SHOOTING SCRIPT® SERIES INCLUDE:

State and Main: The Shooting Script
Gods and Monsters: The Shooting Script
American Beauty: The Shooting Script
Snow Falling on Cedars: The Shooting Script
The Truman Show: The Shooting Script
Man on the Moon: The Shooting Script
The Ice Storm: The Shooting Script
Dead Man Walking: The Shooting Script
The Birdcage: The Shooting Script
The Shawshank Redemption: The Shooting Script
The People vs. Larry Flynt: The Shooting Script
The Age of Innocence: The Shooting Script

OTHER NEWMARKET PICTORIAL MOVIEBOOKS AND NEWMARKET INSIDER FILM BOOKS INCLUDE:

*Crouching Tiger, Hidden Dragon: A Portrait of Ang Lee's Epic Film**
Gladiator: The Making of the Ridley Scott Epic Film
*Stuart Little: The Art, the Artists and the Story Behind the Amazing Movie**
The Jaws Log
*Cradle Will Rock: The Movie and the Moment**
Saving Private Ryan: The Men, The Mission, The Movie
Amistad: A Celebration of the Film by Steven Spielberg
*The Seven Years in Tibet Screenplay and Story**
*Men in Black: The Script and the Story Behind the Film**
*The Age of Innocence: A Portrait of the Film**
*The Sense and Sensibility Screenplay & Diaries**
*Mary Shelley's Frankenstein: The Classic Tale of Terror Reborn on Film**
*Bram Stoker's Dracula: The Film and the Legend**
*Dances with Wolves: The Illustrated Story of the Epic Film**
The Inner Circle: An Inside View of Soviet Life Under Stalin
*Neil Simon's Lost in Yonkers: The Illustrated Screenplay of the Film**

**Includes Screenplay*

CONTENTS

ABOUT THE DIRECTOR AND SCREENWRITERS

NEIL LABUTE (Director)Neil LaBute is a graduate of Brigham Young University, The University of Kansas, and New York University. While enrolled in the Graduate Dramatic Writing Program at NYU, he was the recipient of a literary fellowship to study at the Royal Court Theatre in London, and also attended the Sundance Institute's Playwrights Lab.

His first feature, *In the Company of Men*, won the Filmmakers Trophy at the 1997 Sundance Film Festival, as well as the New York Film Critics Circle's Award for Best First Feature; and went on to become a hit with critics and audiences in its theatrical release. For his script, LaBute was honored with the Best First Screenplay Award at the Independent Spirit Awards.

LaBute's second feature, *Your Friends & Neighbors*, premiered in 1998 and also found success with critics and audiences. The film starred Amy Brenneman, Aaron Eckhart, Catherine Keener, Nastassja Kinski, Jason Patric, and Ben Stiller.

His plays include "Filthy Talk for Troubled Times," "Rounder," "Sanguinarians & Sycophants," and "Ravages." He also penned adaptations of "Dracula" and "Woyzeck," which have been produced at venues in this country and abroad.

JOHN C. RICHARDS (Story and Screenplay) *Nurse Betty* is based on an original short story by John C. Richards. At this year's Cannes International Film Festival, Richards and James Flamberg shared the Best Screenplay award for *Nurse Betty*.

In addition to writing over 60 short stories, Richards has written for other mediums. His first produced film screenplay was for the Canadian feature *Obstruction of Justice*, and he is currently writing *Pen Pals*, for Material Films, at Warner Bros.

His stage play "The Picnic Basket" was produced by the West Coast Theater Ensemble. He has also written the television documentaries "In Search of Angels" (for ABC) and "Gardens of the World" (for PBS); and is currently at work on a novel.

JAMES FLAMBERG (Screenplay) At this year's Cannes International Film Festival, James Flamberg shared the Best Screenplay award for *Nurse Betty*, which is his first produced feature film screenplay. Flamberg also brings to the film expertise from another of his film industry trades: music producing and editing.

Flamberg's association with Baltimore Pictures principals Gail Mutrux (later producer of *Nurse Betty*) and (filmmaker) Barry Levinson dates back to his work as music editor on *Good Morning Vietnam*, *Rain Man*, and *Avalon*. Subsequently, on *Bugsy*, he served as not only executive music producer but also as additional editor. After working as music supervisor on *Toys*, Flamberg associate-produced *Jimmy Hollywood* and *Disclosure* (on which he was also music editor).

His other film work as music editor includes *The Color Purple*, *The Milagro Beanfield War*, *Field of Dreams*, *Black Rain*, *Bird on a Wire*, *Maverick*, and *Toy Story*.

Following *Nurse Betty*, Flamberg completed two screenplays as writing assignments with John C. Richards. Flamberg has recently completed writing two new feature film screenplays: an original thriller, and an adaptation of William Wharton's novel *Franky Furbo*.

INTRODUCTION

BY NEIL LaBUTE

SILENCE. DARKNESS.

SLOW FADE UP ON:

A blinking computer cursor. Bright, incessant. Think HAL from *2001*, without the reasonable voice. GO WIDE to see NEIL LABUTE, late 30's, larger than one might imagine he'd be (but big-boned rather than overweight), plaid shirt, canvas utility pants, faded pumas. GO WIDER. . . he's really big boned.

LaBute is perched on the edge of a chair in the only air-conditioned office at Shepperton Studios, desperate to write an introduction to the soon-to-be-published script of his latest film, *Nurse Betty*. He is snacking, although he stubbornly continues to call them "chips" rather than "crisps," leading to much harping from those around him. He shifts in his seat again, glancing at

THE COMPUTER SCREEN

in front of him. Cursor still blinking dully. No help there.

NEIL

> . . . so, so, so. This should be simple. It's an Intro, for heaven's sake, most people will skip right past it, or think it's a publishing error. Errant script pages, mistakenly placed up front. That would be embarrassing. . . well, at least they won't blame it on me. Okay, okay, come on now. . . think. Or at least write. They don't always go together. . .

He reaches for another chip, or crisp, or whatever the hell it is, munches it quietly. Begins again.

NEIL (CONT'D)

> Just put something down. . . something nice about the guys,

(CONTINUED)

how much you enjoyed the thing when you first read it, loved the spirit of it, and all that stuff. . . be graceful, simple. Truthful. Or at least kind. "Kind" is good, people like "kind," don't they? More than they like "truth," probably. . . most of the time. Not like Hitler kissing babies "kind," because people can see through that, but true kindness, from the heart sort of thing. Right, okay. . . so just do it!

LaBute moves off again, this time snapping open a Diet Pepsi with one hand (fairly clever) and plopping back down to the task. Nothing's coming. That damn cursor!

NEIL (CONT'D)

It's true, though. . . I really did enjoy "Nurse Betty" the first time I read it. So, that's not a big fib. Good, start with that. . . "I really liked it." Perfect. It's a start. We can change it later. . . make it seem like the story was your idea if you get on "The Tonight Show." It wasn't though, it was all theirs, John C. Richards and James Flamberg. John's story, I guess, and then written as a team. First script, too, as I understand it. . . Good God, "best screenplay" at Cannes, right off the bat. (suddenly a touch jealous) I did a lot of work on the dialogue. . . I should've just taken the script and put my name on it, like in "Deathtrap." Yea, but then I'd have to invite the guys over and strangle them, plus buy a country house to do the deed at. . . no, too much work. Damn it!!

LaBute slaps himself back to reality. . . not so much a physical slap, really, as a gentle tap to remind himself that people will find him odd if found talking to himself. . .

NEIL (CONT'D)

Okay, alright. . . we've been through this. It's their script, not yours. The plot hasn't really been altered, the characters are all theirs. . . there's no way around it. Just because you like something doesn't make it yours. How did your mother raise you, anyway? True, true. That's why you were drawn to it in the first place, remember? Because you <u>didn't</u> write it. . . but could you do it? Bring someone else's vision to life, juggle the tone, deal with a female protagonist, get paid more than ever before? Or at least get paid? All important questions. . .

(CONTINUED)

The phone RINGS. Someone looking for the Art Department. LaBute is perfectly nice, courteous even, but loses the call in the transfer. The cursor blinks again, catching his eye.

NEIL (CONT'D)

Okay, already. . . what else? Should say something about Gail Mutrux and Steve Golin bringing the thing to my attention, their tireless efforts to bring it to the screen. That'd be nice for them, they did a lot of work and it's nice to see your name in print. . . so I'll definitely do that. "Gail and Steve were very instrumental in the creation of the picture." Yes, that sounds excellent! Another few lines and I'll be done. . . it would be nice to mention other folks, too, while I'm at it, Phillip and Steven (both of them) and Lynette and Charles and Jean Yves and Melissa and Rolfe and Frankie and Albert and Heidi and Joel and Zac and the actors, Renée and Morgan and Chris and Greg (those I would need to keep in contractual order if I use them) and Aaron and all the rest, so many people. . . and we're all here because of the birth of that single idea which became the film. Maybe I should do that. . . no, it's getting a bit "New Age-y" and it looks like filler. Forget it. . . have them add a credit list at the end. Much better. Much more professional.

SOME WORKERS are building a set outdoors, the NOISE level slowly growing as they dig into it with electric tools. LaBute watches them for a moment, glances back to the screen. The cursor. Hypnotic.

NEIL (CONT'D)

Anything else? God no. . . I'm rambling! Just wrap it up, a cute exit and you're off. No one can hold you responsible if you make a cute exit. . . Was I trying to say anything with the film? Make a comment about the way reality and fantasy can so easily bend to our will, or bend us to its will? Point out that sometimes we have to go a little crazy to find ourselves? Probably, but nobody'll listen to that crap. . . don't even bring it up! I better call John and Jim and see if they have a quick theme or two I can mention, just to sound a bit smarter. . . mental note to self. "Appear brighter in public."

(CONTINUED)

LaBute YAWNS, stretching his big-boned frame out expansively.

NEIL (CONT'D)

> That's it. Finished. . . hope they like it. Or at least don't call asking for more thematic stuff. Hell, I don't know. . . I did it because I liked it, why else would you do something? Thank goodness for Cannes. . . nothing like a nice award from an international jury to fall back on when justifying your creative decisions. "Nurse Betty" exists because it deserves to exist. . . it's clever and fun and sweet and romantic and madcap and frightening and provocative. For me, that's enough. Somehow, miraculously, it made it's way through the system. . .

He hits "SAVE," deciding to cut his losses and simply walk away. It's not going to get any better than this. It must be time for lunch, anyway. . . He glances back once, notices the cursor, ever watching. It winks at him. He smiles.

SILENCE. DARKNESS.

BY JOHN C. RICHARDS AND JAMES FLAMBERG

JOHN C. RICHARDS

First came a drawing in a sketchbook. A profile of a vaguely futuristic nurse called Betty. Then came a short story based on a real nurse, a gargantuan woman who worked at a nursing home in Rochester, N.Y., where I spent a summer as a groundskeeper. She was a sex object, and knew it, because there were men on the staff who liked their nurses big. Then came a treatment that was the real blueprint for the script that would become *Nurse Betty*, the movie. The only thing these three incarnations had in common was their title.

The Betty of the treatment came from the Midwest, watched David Ravell on his soap opera obsessively and was ripe for a delusional experience if the catalyst was strong enough. I have always been drawn to characters who pursue their own insanities in the face of a world that tells them they can't, shouldn't, or better stop doing it right away. In Betty's case, insisting that David was real became the defining mission of the story. Through her "insanity" and her confusion of real and fantasy worlds, she would find a life of her own.

I had been writing short stories for many years and screenplays for a few, and I met Jim Flamberg because he was my next-door neighbor. We collaborated on a spec adaptation of a popular novel and felt that it worked, so when we cast about for another story, Betty's name came up, and he sparked to the treatment immediately.

Jim brings a very strong work ethic and an incredible ability to know when a scene, sequence or movie is working or not, and why. We share a willingness to pursue the truth of each moment in a story, and we were rigorous in hashing out every beat in terms of logic, flow, pace, etc. When we finally sent Betty out into the world, she had already been table-read twice and tested in our little "laboratory" for months. This was 1995.

Jim got Betty to Gail Mutrux, and in her we found the producer who would not only "get" it, but have the stamina to endure the ups and downs of seeing it to production. Some people wouldn't read past the nasty moment that spins Betty into a delusional state; others thought it was "two movies," or "didn't know what it wanted to be." But we knew, and so did Gail and Steve Golin. When they brought Neil LaBute aboard we also knew that we were good hands.

Neil immediately saw what was good about the script and came up with a number of ideas to make it better. When we sat down to work together for the first time he made a short speech that wound up with "Best idea wins," and both Jim and I knew then that we were working with someone who was not only talented, but had integrity and a commitment to the material. He made us welcome on the set, and he was always ready to discuss a scene, a line or a word. Neil made *Nurse Betty* his own, and the end result is that much better for it.

JAMES FLAMBERG

It's all Michele Nieri's Fault—I'm sitting in John's kitchen, we're casting about, trying to find a story idea that would spur us into writing a movie. We'd collaborated on a book adaptation, and liked the experience enough to want to try it again, this time with an original story… We pitched our ideas to each other, but being guys, we couldn't quite say no to the other guy's idea, but we couldn't say yes either… Enter John's wife, Michele. She'd cut through the creative logjam like a buzzsaw. She'd listen to both ideas and make the call… Kind of like the coffee guy who traipses into tiny South American villages, tasting beans. Our lives (at least for the next half year) were riding on her decision.

I went first: something about a letter, a stranger, an obsession, and a long passage of time. John told his: a Kansas nurse comes to believe her favorite soap opera's real, falls in love with the main character, and drives to LA to find him. When I heard John tell it this time, I scratched my head: *why didn't I see that before?* Michele's certainty gave us the courage to commit. With the weight of the decision happily off our shoulders, we both plunged into developing the story…

Come on down and see the new cars at Del Sizemore's—Just thinking about this character always made me laugh. Del became a comic touchstone for me, and later, I'd always know if a scene was working if thinking about the characters, or situation, made me laugh!

He's not really gonna scalp him, is he?—The first big epiphany. In the beginning, we never sat down and said to each other, "Let's write a black comedy," but the total terrain was set with the scalping. Even at the outlining stage, we knew the scene had to be pretty horrific. Functionally, it was the most important scene in the script. It had to believably push a somewhat normal woman into a delusional state. We knew that she would witness the murder of her husband, but how were we gonna kill him? John had a lot of Indian lore in his rucksack, and came up with this horrifyingly funny scene. The scalping became a stylistic beacon, a one-two punch, casting its bi-tonal light, illuminating future twists and turns...

Ballard, Roy, and the Kickapoos—These two nitwits set us firmly on the road of misunderstanding, which motivates every character, and is the recurring motif in the story. In the midst of this horrific crime scene, sheriff Ballard does this bumbling Barney Fife, while the reporter basically solves the case for him. At that point I knew we had something special, something audiences hadn't seen before. The Ballard and Roy scene was a comic launching pad of sorts that said to the reader, beware! These guys are gonna veer from straight drama to balls-out comedy, sometimes within a scene.

Fellow Travelers on the Betty Road—Neil LaBute... "He's not scared of the rough edges in the script!" That's the first thing I thought, after meeting Neil. Watching his two films ("In the Company of Men" and "Your Friends and Neighbors") confirmed that. We dreaded that whoever came aboard as the director could "take it to the center," rounding off those sharp edges, making it more palatable for a larger audience. Neil laid that concern to rest. In fact, he thrived on the "uncomfortable moments," and, in the shooting, made them even more authentic. His casting choices were spot on, and only deepened the emotional pull of the story.

Gail Mutrux and Steve Golin... With producers like these, who needs friends? Even when it seemed like every director in Hollywood wasn't interested, they continued to believe and search. When they found Neil, they then had to talk a studio that was lukewarm about the script into actually making the movie. No mean feat...Gail always kept us in the loop. She made us feel like we were still a vital part of the team, all the way through the production. Not the usual treatment of screenwriters. And it was Steve's stroke of genius to cast Morgan and Chris...

The Gestalt—What stays with me the most is the fun we had writing it. Holed up in John's writing room, cracking each other up. It was collaboration in the best sense of the word, and for that experience, I'll always be grateful.

ON CUTTING STUFF OUT: REFLECTIONS ON A PROCESS

It's amazing what you lose along the way. Sitting here, looking at the script and back on all that was hoped and planned and shot and, on occasion, even edited, one almost can't believe it. But here it is, in your hands. The proof. *Nurse Betty* currently runs about ninety-six minutes. . . the first edited assembly was just under four hours long. And so it goes. You roll up your sleeves, take out your golden axe named "Avid" and get down to business.

As painful a process as it is, most directors love editing. Seeing the picture slowly bump itself together, making connections one never thought possible. Certainly not back when you were writing and shooting. I mean, you're not just doing this just for the fun of it (well, you are but you should never cop to the fact), you've put these things there because you honestly believe you needed them to tell the story. To help explain. But along comes a cast and crew who bless you with their talents and can, magically, turn your sonnets into deeply felt haikus. A glance replaces a monologue. A costume replaces a block of description. And so you continue to hack away.

What remains on screen of John and Jim's first draft is what made it through—not what deserved to, what should have or plain "got lucky." What's left is what tells the story best. As you read, you'll stumble across characters who were severely trimmed back or cut (Chris McDonald's truck driver was a marvel of Midwestern belligerence), scenes that were gutted or lost (Wesley's "doggie-style" interrogation of Joyce and Betty's vaudevillian act as she waited in a doctor's office were particular treats) and clever passages that were pared down or jettisoned altogether (Charlie's musings about his upcoming retirement and George's longing to work in prime-time television are now grace notes rather than subplots). All I can say is, it happens. . . it hurts, it stings and yet you do it. Does it make the work better? Arguably, yes. It gets shorter and funnier and sweeter and scarier and more coherent. But there are those days when you look back fondly on a piece of physical business or a turn of phrase someone used and wish it had remained. Besides, you try telling Chris McDonald that he's been cut from the picture. . . he's even bigger-boned than I am!

So read and enjoy. Read it all and see how we did. Agree, argue or throw this book down in disgust. Better yet, be interactive. You must have scissors around somewhere. . . cut out the bits you don't like. Pick up a pencil and add something in the margins. Go ahead. It's your script now, do as you like.

—Neil LaBute

Nurse Betty

by

John C. Richards
& James Flamberg

Story by

John C. Richards

SHOOTING SCRIPT (FINAL)
3/9/99

FADE IN:

1 INT. OPERATING ROOM - DAY 1

A tense surgery in progress. Meters flicker, instruments flash in the bright overhead light. In the midst of it all stands DR. DAVID RAVELL, 35. The master of his domain. Ravell leans forward so a NURSE can mop the sweat from his brow as he completes a last, delicate procedure. His co-workers sigh collectively with relief.

DAVID
(to Asst. Surgeon)
Close her up, will you?

2 INT. HOSPITAL CORRIDOR - DAY 2

Dr. Ravell comes out of surgery, clearly exhausted. Without his surgical mask he is ruggedly handsome. TWO NURSES follow, attending him like a fighter fresh from the ring: CHLOE, 25, Raven-haired and striking, and JASMINE, 24, an exotic mix of African-American and Asian.

BLAKE DANIELS, 58, the silver-haired Chief Surgeon, rushes up the corridor. On his heels is DR. LONNIE WALSH, 33. Lonnie is also conspicuously handsome, but he'll always be second to David. In everything.

The look on Blake's face stops David in his tracks.

BLAKE
There's been a train crash near Santa Barbara. They're flying an aortal trauma here now. How can I ask you this, David...

David rubs his eyes. Thinks about it.

DAVID
I can do it, Blake.

His bravery isn't lost on the two nurses, although Chloe exchanges a quick, covert glance with Lonnie.

CHLOE
Is he crazy, Jasmine? He's been on his feet for fourteen hours.

JASMINE
Chloe, it's been this way since Leslie died. Losing himself in his work, poor thing...

YOUNGER MAN'S
VOICE
(O.S.)
... I'll give you something to lose yourself in...

OLDER MAN'S VOICE
(O.S.)
Excuse me, miss?

PULL BACK TO REVEAL: WE ARE LOOKING AT A TELEVISION SCREEN BEHIND THE COUNTER OF A SMALL-TOWN DINER.

INSERT: FAIR OAKS, KANSAS

3 INT. TIP TOP DINER - DAY 3

Quaint, Midwestern eatery. Knick-knacks and photos abound. The booths and counter are packed with LOCALS. A family dining section off in one corner.

TWO GUYS sitting at the counter in team jackets. The older of the two holds up his empty coffee cup. But his WAITRESS, standing a couple seats down from him, doesn't move. She's completely absorbed in watching the soap opera that plays on two battered, fuzzy TV sets.

BETTY SIZEMORE, 30, has a wholesome attractiveness that competes with a bit too much makeup and a cheesy white waitress uniform. TWO OTHER WAITRESSES attend to customers behind her.

The younger of the two guys is involved in the soap opera. But the older one, still wants coffee. He gestures toward Betty.

OLDER MAN
Miss?

Betty leans forward, grabs the coffee pot and moves in front of him. Without taking her eyes from the TV, she pours the java, which somehow lands in his cup without spilling a drop.

OLDER MAN
(cont'd)
Very impressive. That is very...
(turning to others)
Did anybody see that?

The LOCAL GUYS around him don't even bother to look up. Of course, they've seen it before. Betty smiles.

OLDER MAN
(cont'd)
Thank you. Could I bother you for a little more...?

Before he can even finish, Betty is topping him off with milk.

BETTY
Skim, right?
(tears open an Equal)
And half a pack, if I remember correct...

The older gentleman's mouth works a bit but nothing comes out. He is flabbergasted by her attention to detail. She looks at the younger man, who is still following the show and gobbling down a huge bacon burger.

BETTY (cont'd)
You know, you're never too young to start on a lean meat substitute...
(BEAT)
You wanna try some turkey bacon on that?

YOUNGER MAN
You want a tip when I'm through?

BETTY
It's your body...

Betty turns back to change pots. The older man watches her intently as the younger of the two mumbles to himself.

YOUNGER MAN
(to himself)
That's right, so why don't you get up off it...

OLDER MAN
Wesley...
(to Betty)
I've told him the same thing. Thanks for the suggestion.

BETTY
No problem.

Betty flashes the men a winning smile and moves off, one eye always on the TV as she approaches two local types.

SHERIFF ELDEN BALLARD, 32, a short, tightly wound little man, sitting at his own booth. Ballard is spit and polish all the way: creases in his shirt, a glossy shine on his shoes. Badge proudly displayed. He sits with

ROY OSTREY, 31, a gangly, bookish local reporter. Betty drops five ketchup packets and four mayonnaise packets on the table for him. Another smile.

ROY
Hi, Betty. You're looking good...

BETTY
Thanks, Roy, you're sweet... a big liar, but sweet. I liked your editorial this morning...

ROY
Oh, appreciate it. I was trying to, ahh, give a sense of history to...

BALLARD
(interrupting)
Yeah, it was great. Really put the whole idea of "church bake sales" in perspective...

ROY
You know, Elden, some people actually read more than just the Classifieds...

BALLARD
Why don't you go back to doing something you're good at... like that Lonelyhearts column?
(chuckles to himself)
I'll take a refill there, Betty...

His cup is full before he can even finish the sentence.

BETTY
Hey, Sheriff. How's everything?

BALLARD
Oh, you know, the usual... keeping the world safe.

BETTY
... I meant your food.

BALLARD
Oh, right... 's fine. Thanks.

ROY
I thought you said the eggs weren't...

BALLARD
It's fine. Mind your own meal...

ROY
You should get the order you want.

BALLARD
And you should keep your nose out of another man's omelette...
(to Betty)
It's no big deal, Betty.

BETTY
There's yolks in there, huh? It's no prob'... gotta keep you on track.

Betty grabs Ballard's plate without another word, gives him a reassuring rub on the shoulders and moves off. He smiles appreciatively after her, then turns on Roy.

BALLARD
Why you always gotta embarrass me? I been eating lunch with you since grade school and you always gotta embarrass me!

ROY
They're just *eggs*, Elden, how embarrassing can eggs be?

BALLARD
... plenty

ROY
Who eats eggs for lunch, anyhow?

BALLARD
Mind your own business. You just said that shit so you could look at her a little longer, anyway...

Still carrying Ballard's plate, she returns to the counter.

BETTY
Come on, guys, I told you it's egg whites only for the Sheriff...
(quietly)
... I put him in that 'zone' thing.

COOK #1
Well, it better be a pretty good size zone if he's in it...

Betty and the cooks share a quick laugh. They move to change his order while Betty glances up at the TV.

4 INT. HOSPITAL CORRIDOR - RETURN TO TV SCREEN 4

Lonnie catches up to Blake in the corridor.

LONNIE
Blake, I can handle that transplant!

BLAKE
We need someone with the right kind of experience, Lonnie.

LONNIE
Even if he's falling asleep on his feet?

BLAKE
Lonnie, it's a complex procedure. Why don't you observe?

LONNIE
I'm not some snot-nosed resident fresh out of medical school, Blake.

BLAKE
No, you're not. You're a good doctor, Lonnie, but you're not David Ravell. I've made my decision. Now, if you'll excuse me ...

Blake exits. The camera moves in to hold on a CLOSEUP of Lonnie's face as he simmers in anger. Music soars.

5 INT. TIP TOP DINER - DAY 5

Plates of food are piling up on the shelf in front of the COOKS. One of them turns the TV off by remote.

BETTY
Hey! We were watching that!

COOK #1
The other girls've got orders up... we're not one 'a them goddamn Nelson families, y'know.

Betty snatches up several plates to help out. Ballard's food appears with A CLATTER of porcelain.

BETTY
It's "Nielson"...

COOK #1
Yeah, well, we ain't one 'a them, neither.
(MORE)

COOK #1 (cont'd)
(BEAT)
Go on now...

DARLENE
When you gonna get those things fixed, anyhow?

COOK #1
When you all quit watching 'em for a living...

Frustrated, Betty delivers several plates and drops them at tables where the people know her by name. She moves off toward FOUR LOCAL GUYS in a booth jangling their empty cups. Betty weaves her way over to them and pours refills. When a hand strays around to touch her ass, she pushes it away with her foot and keeps right on pouring. Absently, Betty takes a look around the restaurant. The other waitresses are gone and no one is behind the grill. Alarmed, she pushes through the double doors into the kitchen.

6 INT. TIP TOP DINER - KITCHEN - SAME TIME 6

THREE WAITRESSES, along with the DISHWASHER and TWO COOKS are standing in a row waiting for her.

BETTY
... alright, I get it, no more TV. Sorry.

No one moves, then DARLENE leads them in a huge SURPRISE! They produce a life-size cardboard cut-out of Dr. David Ravell, who looks dashing in his green hospital scrubs. Betty backs up in disbelief.

BETTY (cont'd)
Oh my gosh, this is so embarrassing! Where did you ever find this?

DARLENE
On the goddamn internet, where else?

BETTY
You're joking...

WAITRESS #1
... nope, got him at "T.V. Hunks with Sweet Little Asses.Com."

WAITRESS #2
Seventy-five dollars...

COOK #1
... Seventy-eight fifty.
(everyone looks at him)
(MORE)

COOK #1 (cont'd)
Well, I paid for the damn thing, I oughta know.

WAITRESS #2
C'mon, Betty! Pose with him!

Betty laughs and puts her arm around the cardboard man. A flash photo is taken. A cupcake with a single candle is placed in her hands.

DARLENE
One candle... uh-oh, you're getting up there! Doesn't David like 'em young?

BETTY
I'm over the hill, what can I say?

Darlene gives Betty an envelope with cash showing.

WAITRESS #1
A little something for those nursing classes you've been wanting to take...

DARLENE
... but keep putting off thanks to a certain husband we won't mention...

BETTY
Oh, guys, you didn't have to do that!

DARLENE
So how you gonna celebrate? Del takin' you into Wichita for a big fancy dinner?

The others laugh; they know better. So does Betty.

BETTY
Yeah, Dairy Queen, maybe... Oh, I should probably call him. Thanks, you guys...

COOK #1
Alright, alright, come on... I'm not running no bed & breakfast, we got customers. Let's go...

Smiling, Betty grabs a wall phone as the others mingle about.

7 INT. SIZEMORE MOTORS - DEL'S OFFICE - DAY 7

The trailer/office of a small-time car dealership. As the PHONE RINGS, the CAMERA PANS across pictures of DEL SIZEMORE, 35, dressed as Napoleon, Caesar and Abe Lincoln, arms raised in a high-energy sales pitch.

The PHONE RINGS again. We see a framed certificate of achievement from General Motors, dated 1986.

After the THIRD RING an ANSWERING MACHINE clicks on. It's loud.

ANSWERING MACHINE
(Del's voice)
Hello there! You've reached Sizemore Motors, home of the best selection of used General Motors cars in the Big Springs - Fair Oaks area. We can't come to the phone right now 'cause we're out making a sale, so leave us a message; better yet, come on down and steal one 'a these beauties right out from under us! Coffee's always on!

BETTY (V.O.)
Hi Del, it's me. I guess you're busy.

8 INT. SIZEMORE MOTORS - TRAILER/OFFICE - DAY 8

Del's very busy. He's on the rented sofa in the trailer's lounge, screwing his secretary, JOYCE. But as he rocks the couch, he's listening to Betty's message.

BETTY (V.O.)
I know you want the Oldsmobile back tonight, so... I was wondering if I could take one of the new Buicks.

Del pulls out and lurches across the room. He reaches for the desk phone but misses, spilling down onto the carpet. He gathers himself and his pants up in disgust, pawing around the desktop until he finds the phone.

BETTY (V.O.)
So, call me when you--

DEL
Whoa, whoa, whoa! Hang on a second there, baby. Why do you need one of the new Buicks?

BETTY (V.O.)
Oh, you're there. You sound out of breath.

DEL
I ran back in to get the phone.

The answering machine is on, so their VOICES are BOOMING. The phone cord is stretched across the trailer as he tries to get back to Joyce. He motions for her to join him but she remains where she is, fuming.

BETTY (V.O.)
I don't *need* one, but it's kind of a special night, and--

DEL
What's so special about it?

LONG PAUSE. Joyce looks at Del, incredulous. Then pissed off. He signals to hold on.

BETTY (V.O.)
Sue Ann's taking me out and I thought it might be fun to go in a nice car...

Joyce wriggles to a sitting position and begins to pull up her panties. Del shoots her a look that says 'I'm not finished yet!' They pantomime frantically back and forth until Joyce throws him the finger and SLAMS out the door.

BETTY (V.O)
What was that?

DEL
Nothing... it's, ahh, busy here. Look, you don't need a LeSabre to go out with Sue Ann. Take the blue Corsica. I'll see you when I get home.

He throws the phone onto the cradle, then bangs on a window to get Joyce's attention as she fires up a smoke.

DEL
(through the pane)
Shit! Joyce, open the damn gate, will you?!

As Del zips up his pants Joyce trudges across the lot to bring in the "Closed For Lunch" sign and open the gate. Del silently studies the much nicer car lot next door for a moment. He takes in the banners, the signs, etc.

DEL (cont'd)
... that's what we need, some goddamn flags.

9 INT. OFFICE/TRAILER - LATER 9

Betty enters the office. Joyce is on the phone. She looks up, irritated, and says something under her breath to the caller.

JOYCE
Uhh, no, we haven't picked a date yet... well, once he dumps her we will.
(to Betty)
He's out pricing banners... I don't expect him back.

BETTY
"Banners?"

JOYCE
You know, flags and shit... he said "for a livelier look" or something.

Betty nods and swaps her car keys for a set Joyce gives her.

JOYCE (cont'd)
'S too bad about the LeSabres... they're a really sweet ride.

As Joyce prattles on, Betty notices the Buick LeSabre keys on a rack behind her. She sidles around Joyce, deftly removes a set from the hook and drops them in her purse. She smiles and starts to wave goodbye as Joyce puts her call on hold.

JOYCE (cont'd)
Need something else?

BETTY
No, I was just... How you doing?

JOYCE
Great. Good. Content...

BETTY
Oh. How come?

JOYCE
I dunno. Job satisfaction, I guess...
(BEAT)
How's things at the Tip Top?

BETTY
They're fine... you miss it?

JOYCE
You must be joking.

BETTY
Hmm.
(BEAT)
So, Del get that car he sold you up and running yet?

JOYCE
Oh, yeah, he's got things up and running, alright...

BETTY
'Kay, good. Bye, then...

JOYCE
Uh-huh.
(back to phone)
Anyway, I'm thinking Easter, 'cause I just fucking love pastels.

She whispers, then laughs loudly as Betty leaves.

10 EXT. SIZEMORE MOTORS - DAY 10

The cardboard doctor is standing next to Betty's Olds. She thinks about leaving him, but picks him up and tosses him into a blue Corsica. He lands with his face against the passenger window.

She stands for a moment by the Corsica, dangling the LeSabre keys before her eyes. Suddenly, she jumps inside the Chevrolet and slams the door.

11 EXT. SIZEMORE MOTORS/TRAILER PARK - DAY 11

The blue Corsica leaves the parking lot and pulls onto the street. The car makes an abrupt turn into a trailer park directly behind the car lot and glides to a halt behind a row of battered airstreams.

Betty gets outs of the Chevy and looks back: the handsome face of Doctor David Ravell is staring at her from the car.

BETTY
Oh, Christ, what am I gonna do with you?

She goes back to pick him up, then starts off.

12 EXT. TRAILER PARK - SAME TIME 12

A row of cheap trailers on both sides of a crumbling driveway. Betty appears with her cardboard man tucked under one arm and then disappears behind a pickup truck.

13 EXT. SIZEMORE MOTORS - SAME TIME 13

She tosses the cardboard "David" over a concrete slab wall, climbs over herself and walks straight to the LeSabres. Her key opens the last one - maroon. She puts the doctor on the passenger seat, gets in the car and inhales the new car smell.

Joyce can be seen inside the trailer, still talking on the phone. She misses the whole scene as she works on her nails.

BETTY
We deserve this.

14 INT. LESABRE - DRIVING - DAY 14

Betty has the car at 75 m.p.h., on the rural Kansas roads, wheat fields for miles on both sides of her. The RADIO is blasting Bonnie Raitt and she's singing along.

She sees her speed and punches the accelerator ... 80 m.p.h. ... 85 ... 90 m.p.h. She turns the radio up louder.

When she approaches a sign saying "You are leaving Kansas" Betty suddenly becomes self-conscious. She eases up on the gas ... slows down ... does a U-turn and heads back toward Fair Oaks. She glances wistfully in her rear view mirror at the billboard that quickly fades into the distance.

15 EXT. BETTY'S NEIGHBORHOOD - LATER 15

Betty enters a modest residential neighborhood and pulls into a driveway. She parks in a detached garage and looks over at the cardboard David. There's no way he's going in the house. She puts him in the trunk and closes the garage door.

16 EXT. SUE ANN'S HOUSE - SAME TIME 16

She walks several houses down. On her way to the door we hear a DOG BARKING, CHILDREN and GENERAL COMMOTION from inside. SUE ANN ROGERS answers Betty's knock. Her hair is matted with sweat as she struggles with CHILDREN, ages 4, 3 and 6 months. Suddenly, Sue Ann is hit by an errant rubber ball.

SUE ANN
Hey, darling... oww! Sorry, got my own little Gulf War going on here.

Betty takes the baby as Sue Ann pulls a videotape from a shelf. It's all one move; they do this every day.

BETTY
Did you watch it yet?

SUE ANN
Sure did. I'll tell you, if that man was any better looking it'd be a crime 'a some sort...

BETTY
Yep. Hey, I got a surprise for tonight. We're going to the Starlite in style!

SUE ANN
Oh, Betty--

BETTY
I'll give you a hint. If you scrunch up your eyes a bit it looks just like a Jaguar...

SUE ANN
Honey, I'm really sorry, I was gonna call you about tonight. Larry's got a lodge meeting. There's no way I can get a sitter this fast.

BETTY
(disappointed)
No... what about your sister?

SUE ANN
I can't ask her again-- Nathan, stop it! Jesse, don't take that, hit back!-- I feel terrible, hon.

After a beat ...

BETTY
It's all right.

SUE ANN
You sure? Maybe next week we could...

BETTY
Uh-huh. No, we'll do it later. 'S only a birthday, right? I'll have another one next year...

Betty forces a smile, kisses the baby and hands it back to Sue Ann, who hands her the videotape.

SUE ANN
Aahhh...
(BEAT)
So what color is it?

BETTY
What?

SUE ANN
The LeSabre!

BETTY
Maroon.
(BEAT)
I stole it.

SUE ANN
What?

BETTY
He wasn't going to let us use it, so I just took it.

SUE ANN
Oh, I wish we could just get in it and drive, and drive, and drive!

BETTY
Yeah, me too.

SUE ANN
Sorry, hon. Happy Birthday...

BETTY
I gotta go make dinner.

Betty throws her a look as Sue Ann closes the door. Betty turns around, frustrated. She starts yanking her apron off as she crosses the street.

17 INT. BETTY'S HOUSE - DAY 17

A low-end ranch. A worn-out sofa and loveseat form an 'L' that dominates the living room. Romance novels line a small bookcase. SIX CANARIES in cages chatter away in the kitchen.

Del sits at the dining room table, agitated. He is presently attacking a pork chop, baked beans and a loaf of Wonderbread. All we hear is A FORK CLICKING and BIRDS CHIRPING. Betty stands at the breakfast counter, barefoot, still in her uniform and quietly eating a salad.

BETTY
Sure you don't want any salad?

DEL
No, I do not want any goddamn... what was all that shit on the phone about the new Buicks?

BETTY
I told you. Sue Ann was gonna take me out tonight, but...

DEL
She's not comfortable in a *Corsica*? 'S got air and leather...

BETTY
I took the blue Corsica, Del. Relax.

DEL
All right, then. Actually, I'm glad you're going out. I got something going on tonight. Some *serious* clients, with *real* potential.

Del BELCHES, smiles, then CLUCKS at the birds nearby.

BETTY
... like the water purifiers?

DEL
What?

BETTY
Or the vitamins? Or the...?

Del almost comes out of his chair, pointing his finger at her.

DEL
Hey, the FDA screwed me on that when they changed the law, and you know it!
(BEAT)
Anyway, 'least I try shit, still got some dreams left... you're a goddamn *waitress*, what do you got?

BETTY
I got you, Del...

DEL
... well, then you ain't got much.

BETTY
Oh, I know.
(BEAT)
So, who're these clients?

DEL
Couple 'a guys in from outta town. They want to see the new LeSabres.

Betty hides her reaction.

DEL (cont'd)
And I don't need Sue Ann's fat ass around to fuck it up...

BETTY
Just knock it off, 'kay? Anyhow, they're 97's, they're not even new.

DEL
They're new to us...

Truce for a moment. Del plucks a copy of *Soap Opera Guide* from Betty's purse while absently taking a bite from Betty's cupcake. He narrowly misses the candle.

DEL (cont'd)
Jesus... you know these actors are mainly models, which are mainly fags. They've done studies. The rest're assholes. But you know what bugs me most about these soaps?

She silently mimics him as he says...

DEL (cont'd)
It's people with no lives watching other people's *fake* lives.

BETTY
Yeah, I guess there's nothing like watching those tenpins fall, huh, Del?

DEL
That is a skill!

Del lurches to his feet and crosses to the bird cages as the canaries CHIRP and SING EXCITEDLY at his approach.

DEL (cont'd)
Daddy's here, babies... daddy's here.
(to Betty)
Be back later... clean up.

He exits. She collects his dirty dishes, puts them in the sink and starts to wash them. Then she stops.

BETTY
What the hell am I doing?

She drops the dishes with a clatter, pours herself a glass of wine, lights the candle on her deflowered cupcake and opens the one card on the table.

CLOSE ON

a traditional greeting from her grandparents. Red hearts and lace. A color photo of them enclosed.

Betty smiles at this. After moment, she quietly sings a quick refrain of "Happy Birthday" to herself.

18 INT. LONNIE'S APARTMENT - NIGHT (ON TV SCREEN) 18

Standing wrapped only in a towel, Lonnie speaks into the phone.

LONNIE
Tell me something good, Sugar.

19 INT. CHLOE'S APARTMENT - NIGHT (ON TV SCREEN) 19

The beautiful nurse Chloe is curled up seductively on her sofa with her phone in one hand and a cigarette in the other.

CHLOE
We're all set. I told him my car's in the shop. He said he'd be happy to give me a ride home.

LONNIE
(V.O.)
You're beautiful.

CHLOE
Tell me something I don't know...

Betty hits FAST FORWARD. Characters flit on and off the screen at top speed until David Ravell appears.

20 INT. WOODED ROADSIDE - NIGHT (ON TV SCREEN) 20

Chloe's magnificent legs are folded into the seat of David's 560 SL. She struggles with her seatbelt, so he helps her. She makes sure their hands touch.

CHLOE
Thanks for pulling over, David... I can't go that fast without taking a breather.

DAVID
Sorry... it's nice to see what this little beauty can do, though. I guess, somehow, all that speed helps me forget the past...

CHLOE
I'm sure it does...
(touching the seats)
Mmm, leather. How far do they recline?

David smiles, a little uncomfortable.

CHLOE (cont'd)
Listen, David, I know I've said it before, but I want to tell you again how sorry I am about your wife.
(BEAT)
It must make you scared to get close to someone again.

She puts her hand over his on the gear shift. A moment. Finally, he has to move her fingers to start the car.

CHLOE (cont'd)
Let's not go... not yet.

BETTY sits on an old couch in the den and watches, eyes glued to the screen. Suddenly, she hears the sound of TIRES ON GRAVEL. HEADLIGHTS sweep across the window.

BETTY
Damn!

She hits PAUSE and crosses to look out.

21 EXT. BETTY'S HOUSE - NIGHT 21

Del gets out of a black Lincoln Town Car, followed by CHARLIE and WESLEY - the guys in the team jackets from the diner. Charlie is 63 years old. He wears a dress shirt, slacks and docksiders. The suburban father look.

Wesley is 28. He's in jeans, T-shirt and white Reeboks. Clean-cut; the kid who used to mow your parents' lawn.

Betty quickly snaps out the light and closes the door until it is open only a crack.

22 INT. BETTY'S HOUSE - NIGHT 22

Del swaggers into the house. The two men follow politely.

DEL
... you can have the best damn running backs in the world, somebody's still gotta block for 'em.

CHARLIE
You're a hundred percent right. They rely on what's-his-name's arm too much...

Del stops and looks around, deflated by the mess.

The den is only a short flight of steps from the living room and the kitchen. Betty has a clean view of both from where she sits on the couch.

23 INT. BETTY'S HOUSE - DEN - NIGHT 23

She hears Del come in, but doesn't take her eyes off the TV screen.

DEL (O.S.)
My apologies, gentlemen. I asked my wife to straighten this shit up before she went out.

23A INT. BETTY'S HOUSE - LIVING ROOM - NIGHT 23A

Del crosses to an old stereo and puts on an LP. He smiles as the music overtakes the room. Charlie and Wesley stand nearby, appreciating the quaintness of the surroundings.

DEL
Now, what can I get you gentlemen to drink?

Del crosses to the cupboard. Charlie and Wesley stand leisurely in the living room.

CHARLIE
Bourbon, little water, thank you.

WESLEY
Beer, please.

DEL
You got it.

Wesley looks at a wedding portrait of Del and Betty.

WESLEY
Hey... you got a fine one right here!

CHARLIE
Wesley...
(to Del)
Your wife's a very lovely woman. Have I seen her before?

DEL
If you ate at the Tip Top you did.

CHARLIE
Oh, yes, with the coffee...

DEL
Yep, Betty pours a pretty mean cup.

Del reaches into the fridge and produces a Miller for Wesley, then mixes two drinks and walks into the dining room and Charlie and Wesley follow to the table and sit down.

CHARLIE
I like this. I like doing business in the home. It's cozy...
(noticing the card and cupcake)
Who's birthday?

DEL
Ahh... my wife's.

WESLEY
What'd you get her?

DEL
Huh? Oh, umm, a car.
(BEAT)
So, to a successful transaction...

They raise their glasses and drink. Del tosses back his drink in one gulp.

24 INT. DAVID'S CAR - WOODED ROADSIDE - (ON TV SCREEN) 24

Chloe is on top of David, kissing him on the mouth as he resists. He finally has to push her away forcibly, and we hear a TEARING SOUND. Chloe's blouse has been ripped.

DAVID
I'm sorry, Chloe.

She starts to cry. David reaches out to comfort her.

DAVID (cont'd)
It's not that I don't find you attractive. I'm just not ready...

David looks up to find her lips on his. In spite of himself, he gives in to the warmth of her kiss and responds hungrily.

Betty is mesmerized.

25 INT. BETTY'S HOUSE - DINING ROOM - NIGHT 25

The men have retired into the dining room, sitting or standing around a worn wooded table. Charlie and Wesley are just finishing their drinks.

DEL
All right gentlemen, let's get down to it. I need to know if you're for real.

CHARLIE
If we're for real?

DEL
You don't exactly look like drug dealers.

WESLEY
Isn't that the point?

DEL
Yeah, well, I don't have time to screw around. I got buyers in Dallas, Houston and Vegas who are ready to snap this stuff up.

CHARLIE
We appreciate that. But you just poured me a drink, I'd like to enjoy your hospitality for a few minutes.

DEL
Fine. You got five...

CHARLIE
It's a nice place you got here. Real comfortable. Sweet little town, Fair Oaks. You like it here?

DEL
(laughs)
Are you kidding me? What's to like?

WESLEY
Seems like a nice place.

DEL
It is, if you like idiots...

CHARLIE
What do you mean?

DEL
It's a small town, man. I never should have left Omaha. People here think
(MORE)

DEL (cont'd)
small. They act small. They're a bunch of dumb fucks.

WESLEY
Really?

DEL
You better believe it.

CHARLIE
Could you give us an example?

DEL
Of what?

CHARLIE
I'm asking you for an example of one of these dumb fucks being a dumb fuck.

DEL
I don't follow...

CHARLIE
You're not a dumb fuck, are you, Del?

DEL
(warily)
No...

CHARLIE
I didn't think so. So, give me an example of a stupid person doing a stupid thing. Not being stupid, you're equipped to recognize it.

DEL
Are we gonna do business here, or not?

WESLEY
Relax, we brought the cash.

CHARLIE
I'm just curious. Can't you give me an example?

DEL
(annoyed)
All right ... lemme see ... okay, new Burger King opens up. These assholes get excited and start lining up. Like it's some five star restaurant. The place is mobbed. Right?

CHARLIE
Hmmmm. "Five Stars," huh?
(BEAT)
Is that stupid, Wesley?

WESLEY
No, that's ignorant. They just don't know any better.

CHARLIE
That's what I thought.
(to Del)
You better give me another example.

DEL
This is bullshit, can we get down to business here, please?

Off a look from Charlie, Wesley produces a pistol and gently nudges the barrel into Del's ear.

DEL
Jesus Christ!

WESLEY
He's waiting...

DEL
Okay, uh... the, umm, Injuns're stupid.

WESLEY
"Injuns?"

CHARLIE
You did not just say "Injuns," Del.

DEL
The Indians, Injuns, whatever. They're always drunk and doing stupid things.

CHARLIE
Like what?

DEL
Driving their cars into trees... puking on the sidewalk... stupid shit!

CHARLIE
Let's see... around here that would be Kiowa, Kickapoo or Osage, if I'm not mistaken.

DEL
I... I don't know...

CHARLIE
Well, my idea of stupid is very different from yours.
(BEAT)
So here's how this is gonna work. Would you take your socks off, please?

DEL
My socks?

WESLEY
You heard the man.

Del slowly takes his shoes and socks off. He's sweating, trembling.

CHARLIE
I'm gonna talk to you and when I'm finished, you can answer. But I don't like being interrupted. Now roll them into a ball...

Del does it.

DEL
Oh, Jesus, please... Please, God.

CHARLIE
... and put them in your mouth.

At a sharp look from Charlie, Del obediently stuffs the socks into his mouth and starts to cry. Wesley produces a roll of duct tape and fastens Del's hands to the back of his chair.

26 INT. BETTY'S HOUSE - DEN - NIGHT 26

Betty is glued to the TV, oblivious to the men. Chloe and David are still talking in his car. She continues to cry.

DAVID
(V.O.)
You're wonderful, Chloe, you are... But I just know there's something special out there for me.

27 INT. BETTY'S HOUSE - DINING ROOM - NIGHT 27

CHARLIE
Now I'm gonna tell you what stupid is. Stupid is taking something that doesn't belong to you. Right Wesley?

WESLEY
That's right.

CHARLIE
Stupid is trying to sell it to other people who are, by their very nature, untrustworthy.

WESLEY
That is so right.

CHARLIE
Stupid is calling people in Kansas City who are affiliated with the rightful owners of the thing you stole, and trying to sell it to them. Right Wesley?

WESLEY
Now, that's really stupid.

CHARLIE
So you see, we have totally different ideas of what's stupid and what's not. Don't we?

Del nods; crying, sweating.

CHARLIE (cont'd)
Good. Now we're getting somewhere. You agree that you were stupid?

Del nods again. Wesley collects Charlie's glass and mixes him another drink. He gets a beer for himself and stands behind Del. Charlie sips his drink slowly, savoring it.

CHARLIE (cont'd)
You know, a hundred and fifty years ago you'd have been scalped for that remark about Native Americans. Right here where your house is - you'd have been scalped.

WESLEY
Hell of a way to die.

CHARLIE
It wasn't always fatal, Wesley. We could scalp Del right now, and he'd be plenty alive to tell us how it feels.

Del's eyes get huge.

CHARLIE
It's pretty simple, too.
(BEAT)
(MORE)

CHARLIE
First you take a knife and just draw a mark right across the hairline.

Wesley produces a long knife and traces a line across the very top of Del's forehead. Trickles of blood wind their way down his brow. Del is MOANING and PANTING through his socks.

CHARLIE (cont'd)
Hold still, Del, we're just talking here...
(pointing to a spot)
Then you grab a big handful of hair and pull as you cut. It's amazing how easily the scalp comes off.

WESLEY
A mark, huh?

Wesley takes a jab at Del's forehead with his knife, leaving a small cut.

Del starts twitching, rocking back and forth as Wesley grabs a fistful of his hair.

WESLEY (cont'd)
Shut the fuck up! I bleed more than that when I shave...

Del stops moving. He breathes furiously through his nostrils.

CHARLIE
Now. I want to know the particulars of your stupid act: how you got what doesn't belong to you, who helped you get it, and of course, where it is now.

Charlie pulls the socks out of Del's mouth. Del splutters, gasping for air.

DEL
It's in the Buick! I swear to God it's all there!

28 INT. BLAKE DANIELS' OFFICE - DAY (ON TV SCREEN) 28

David enters. Blake nods to him grimly.

DAVID
You wanted to see me, Blake?

BLAKE
I wish I could say I had good news.
(off David's look)
David, I'll get right to the point. Chloe Jensen has filed charges of sexual
(MORE)

BLAKE (cont'd)
assault against you.
(BEAT)
You can continue to practice at L.A. County, but I'm afraid I have to revoke your privileges here at Loma Vista until this is resolved.

HOLD on David's shocked expression ... MUSIC UP AS

DEL (O.S.)
PLEASE DON'T KILL ME!!!

Betty's not sure what Del said, but the panic in his voice got through. She hits PAUSE and takes a look.

29 INT. BETTY'S HOUSE - DINING ROOM - NIGHT 29

Del is facing her, tiny rivulets of blood running into his terrified eyes. Wesley stands at his shoulder, still holding a handful of his hair, still poised with the knife.

DEL
I got it from a truck driver named Duane Cooley, out of Amarillo. He brings my cars down from Detroit. But I haven't touched it, I swear to you... Please! Please! Please!

Annoyed, Charlie stuffs the socks back in Del's mouth.

Betty stares. Her gaze shifts from Del to Wesley, drawn by Wesley's demonic expression.

CHARLIE
Consider yourself lucky. Luckier than those 'Injuns' you have such contempt for.

Wesley stares at the top of Del's head. Betty stares at Wesley. Charlie walks into the kitchen for another drink.

CHARLIE (cont'd)
I'll tell you, if anyone got a raw deal it's the American Indian. This country has a black mark on its soul for what was done to them.

Wesley's nostrils flare. Betty leans forward.

CHARLIE (cont'd)
I'm all for them owning casinos, getting rich off the white man's greed. It's a beautiful piece of irony, isn't it, Wesley?

WESLEY
IT SURE IS!!

And with a long SCREAM, Wesley rips Del's scalp from his head. It makes a sickening sound like fabric tearing. For a long moment, there is only silence. An eerie silence.

Suddenly, Del SCREAMS into his socks and thrashes in his seat, blood pouring down his head on all sides.

Somehow, he manages to get to his feet, the chair still taped to him, and begins smashing into whatever is near. Blood flies and curios shatter as Del thunders through the room. A dying bull, only messier. It's quite a show.

CHARLIE
JESUS CHRIST!!!

Wesley steps back, staring at the dripping scalp in his hand, as if wondering how it got there. Betty is transfixed, horrified.

Charlie re-enters. The two men look at each other over Del's MUFFLED SCREAMS as he plows headlong into wooden paneling, a china cabinet, and finally, back toward them near the breakfast counter. Del bashes blindly into it.

CHARLIE (cont'd)
(to Wesley)
What the fuck is the matter with you?!

Wesley is practically foaming at the mouth, still rushing on what he did. Charlie draws a silenced pistol and mercifully SHOOTS Del through the head. The big man stops suddenly, blinks once or twice, topples over.

30 INT. BETTY'S HOUSE - DEN - NIGHT 30

Betty points her remote at the dining room and clicks it, as if trying to make the image disappear. Finally, she gives up, slowly turning away from the carnage and aims at the TV. "A Reason to Love" pauses on the face of David Ravell and Betty sits in absolute silence.

31 INT. BETTY'S HOUSE - DINING ROOM - NIGHT 31

Charlie quickly begins to hide their tracks, producing a plastic baggie and collecting the beer cans and his own glass. He also wipes down the fridge as Wesley watches.

CHARLIE
Are you out of your mind? You scalped him!

WESLEY
You told me how to do it!

CHARLIE
That was to get him to talk!
(BEAT)
Get rid of that thing, will you?

Wesley crosses to the garbage can, steps on the lever. He looks at the scalp one more time before dropping it in.

CHARLIE
This is great - just great! Now we don't know where the goddamn stuff is.

WESLEY
He told us it's in the Buick.

CHARLIE
We don't know which Buick, do we?

WESLEY
Well, why'd you shoot him?

CHARLIE
I had to shoot him! It was the only decent thing to do.

They exit the house.

CHARLIE (O.S.)
This is very unprofessional, Wesley.

32 INT. BETTY'S HOUSE - DEN - NIGHT 32

Betty is still in the family room, staring at the TV. She pushes 'play' again and David Ravell begins to speak.

33 EXT. SUE ANN'S HOUSE - STREET - LATER 33

Sue Ann comes out of her house, balancing a homemade cake in front of her. The candles give off an unearthly glow as she picks her way up the Sizemore's gravel drive.

34 INT. BETTY'S HOUSE - DEN - SAME TIME 34

Betty is catatonic, staring at the frozen image of David Ravell on her TV. Downstairs, Sue Ann comes in.

SUE ANN
(O.S.)
Happy Birthday to you! Happy Birthday to you! Happy Birthday, dear--

A terrified SCREAM as the cake lands unceremoniously on the entryway.

ON BETTY

As she hits 'Play':

DAVID
... you're wonderful, Chloe, you are... But I just know there's something special out there for me.

35 INT. BETTY'S HOUSE - FOYER - LATER THAT NIGHT 35

Roy enters the foyer and looks around, carrying a pad and pen in hand. He hears VOICES from the kitchen, sees FLASHBULBS going off. He sneaks down the hall when A VOICE stops him.

DEPUTY
Hang on there, Roy. Nobody comes in.

ROY
Elden called me. He wants to, ahh, make a statement for the paper...

The deputy nods him through and Roy moves off toward the sewing room where he has spotted Betty.

36 INT. BETTY'S HOUSE - SEWING ROOM - SAME TIME 36

Betty is packing an overnight bag on her bed when Roy enters and quietly closes the door behind him. She is working with a purpose, almost like a different person from the woman we first met. Still bright and cheerful, but with a willful glint in her eye. Determined.

ROY
Hey, Betty. Are you okay?

BETTY
I'm great, good, content.
(stopping)
What happened to your arm, Roy?

ROY
Oh, nothing, it's fine. I just need to keep it wrapped for a few...

BETTY
Make sure it's elevated...

ROY
Uh-huh.

BETTY
You want me to make you a sling? It's no problem...

Betty starts whipping a T-shirt into place but stops abruptly. She turns curiously to Roy.

BETTY (cont'd)
What're you doing here, Roy?

ROY
Well, I was worried about you and I wanted to make sure you were alright... and I guess I was sort of hoping I could ask you about what happened...

BETTY
Oh, that... Sure, I saw the whole thing. It was disgusting!

ROY
My God... did you get a look at who did it?

BETTY
Yes.

ROY
You *did*? Was it anyone that you...?

BETTY
It was Chloe...

Sheriff Ballard enters the house, surveys the scene of the crime where one deputy wipes blood off his boot with a paper towel, and erupts when he sees Roy.

BALLARD
Hey, you guys wanna try not stepping directly in the evidence, please?
(to Roy)
Ostrey, you and your goddamn police scanner! I leave for ten minutes and... Betty, I'm sorry about this.

He motions to a female officer.

BALLARD (cont'd)
Why don't you take her down to the station? We'll be along in a bit...

She leads Betty out the kitchen door.

BETTY
'Night, guys...

37 INT. BETTY'S HOUSE - DINING ROOM - NIGHT 37

As Ballard leads Roy into the next room...

BALLARD
Okay, let's go... I got nothing for the record yet.

ROY
Oww! My arm, careful!

BALLARD
Ahh, what'd you do now... fall off your bike again?

ROY
No, it's nothing, I... my piranha just mauled me a little when I layed their food out.

BALLARD
Good God...they're *meat eaters*, Roy, just drop the shit in there!

ROY
I can't...they prefer a more formal presentation. I don't usually go so close to the surface, but I was...

BALLARD
...you are so goddamn weird.
(BEAT)
Oh, and by the way, get the hell outta here!

ROY
No, Elden, I need to...

BALLARD
You need to get yourself gone from my crime scene. And leave Betty alone, she's...

ROY
She knows who killed Del. Elden, she said it was a woman.

BALLARD
It wasn't a woman.

ROY
Yes it was. Betty saw the whole thing! Your killer's name is Chloe...

BALLARD
I'm tellin' you it wasn't no woman, Roy!

38 INT. BETTY'S HOUSE - LIVING ROOM - NIGHT 38

Ballard drags Roy into the living room, where he sees Del. He has been turned upright and is being carefully examined.

ROY
Jesus...

BALLARD
You think a woman did *that*?!

Roy runs into the kitchen, covering his mouth.

39 INT. BETTY'S HOUSE - KITCHEN - NIGHT 39

Ballard and his cronies delight in watching Roy struggle with the dry heaves. Roy runs to the kitchen sink, almost loses it, then wipes his mouth with a paper towel.

BALLARD
Kinda' looks like a burnt out roman candle, don't he?
(BEAT)
Del must've sold a lemon to the wrong Indian, and got paid back the old fashioned way. Them Kickapoos get pretty mean when they drink...

Roy sees Del's scalp in the garbage can as he goes to drop his crumpled towel inside.

ROY
So, you think you're gonna find his scalp hanging in some tepee?

BALLARD
They no longer live in tepees, Mr. College Graduate.

ROY
Did you send anyone out there?

BALLARD
You bet I did. I got a squad car on the way to the reservation right now.

ROY
Bad idea ...

BALLARD
You just go write your little story, Roy. I'll handle the police work...

ROY
You better handle what's in this garbage can first.

40 EXT. SIZEMORE MOTORS - NIGHT 40

Every car on the lot has its trunk open and spare tire on the ground behind it. Charlie and Wesley are at the last car.

WESLEY
I still don't understand how you knew Del was telling the truth.

CHARLIE
I saw his soul Wesley. He was face to face with his God, and no one lies in that situation. But your Geronimo act rattled me, and I abandoned my instincts.
(BEAT)
Never abandon you instincts.

WESLEY
I didn't. You gave me a look!

CHARLIE
What 'look'?

WESLEY
That one look you got! I thought you were done, so I took him out...

CHARLIE
I wasn't done, I was just sick of hearing him whine. And you didn't take him out, you scalped him. Christ, I almost puked, did I tell you that?

WESLEY
Well, why'd you have to tell that Indian story?

CHARLIE
What the hell does *that* mean? If I'd told a Ty Cobb story would you have clubbed him to death with a bat?

Wesley is stung. Charlie slams the last trunk in disgust. The rest remain where they are; open.

CHARLIE (cont'd)
It's not here. Let's go.

WESLEY
You just gonna leave these cars sitting here like this?

CHARLIE
Why not, it'll confuse 'em... gotta do something, now that you fucked it up.

WESLEY
I wanted to make a statement.

CHARLIE
Let me tell you something. In our business you can't put food on the table if your phone doesn't ring. The guys who get the calls are good - not flashy, just good. They get in, they get out. Nobody knows a goddamn thing. Understand? Boom, boom, boom. Three in the head and you know they're dead.

WESLEY
... that's a good motto.

CHARLIE
Fine, I'll get you a bumpersticker, but you better start believing it! It's the only *statement* you need to make.

41 INT. POLICE STATION / OBSERVATION ROOM - NIGHT 41

Betty is questioned in a holding room by a POLICE OFFICER and a DOCTOR. Ballard and Roy watch through a window.

DOCTOR
And did your husband know these people?

BETTY
Sort of...but he ignored them.

DOCTOR
And how did that make you feel, Betty?

BETTY
I felt all cold inside. And angry.

Ballard looks both ways to make sure he won't be overheard.

BALLARD
I questioned Joyce about all this...

ROY
Yeah?

BALLARD
Seems she was pretty familiar with 'ol Del. On a regular basis, if you get my drift...

ROY
... and half the other guys in this town. Including you, I believe...

BALLARD
Junior year!

ROY
Anyway, so what?

BALLARD
<u>So</u>? ... Suppose Betty found out about them?

ROY
You said a woman couldn't have done it.

BALLARD
A woman can write a check.

ROY
So you're saying Betty Sizemore - *our* Betty Sizemore--who you were in swing choir with--has now hired somebody to scalp her husband in her own kitchen while she watched? You're amazing.

BALLARD
'S just a theory...just 'cause I'm thinking it don't mean I like it.

The doctor comes out of the holding room.

BALLARD (cont'd)
How is she?

DOCTOR
She's in a kind of shock. I see all the signs of a post-traumatic reaction with possible dissociative symptoms.

BALLARD
Could I have that in American?

DOCTOR
It's a type of altered state...it allows a traumatized person to continue functioning.

BALLARD
So she *did* witness it?

ROY
Oh, you're sharp as a tack, Elden.

BALLARD
That's it! YOU'RE GONE!

He spins Roy around and marches him toward the door, one arm bent behind his back.

ROY
Oww, the arm, the arm!

BALLARD
You just don't know when to quit, Roy! You were jealous of me when I got hall monitor in seventh grade, and you're still jealous now!!!

ROY
One question, Doctor, please! (outside the door) You can't do this! I'm the press, I have rights!!

BALLARD
That's right, you have the right to remain silent.

Ballard pushes Roy out the door. As he returns, Roy reappears behind him, leaning in to listen. Ballard doesn't see him.

BALLARD (cont'd)
Sorry you had to see that. You were saying?

DOCTOR
I was saying that it seems probable that she witnessed the murder, but her memory of it is gone, at least for the time being. I also think you ought to have her
(MORE)

DOCTOR (cont'd)
stay with someone tonight.
(BEAT)
Any idea who Chloe or Lonnie are?

BALLARD
No... Friends from the diner maybe?

DOCTOR
Well, you should find out. She keeps talking about them...

Ballard nods, sure he's got a clue here. He looks in at Betty again, just as she begins repacking her travel bag. He frowns at this, his suspicions fueled all the more.

42 EXT. SUE ANN'S HOUSE - NIGHT 42

A police car pulls up to Sue Ann's house. Betty gets out, carrying her overnight bag. Sue Ann appears, embraces her and leads her inside.

43 INT. SUE ANN'S HOUSE - BEDROOM - LATER 43

Betty lies down in a bright red race car bed. Sue Ann tucks her in and turns out the light.

SUE ANN
Let me know if you need anything, okay?

BETTY
Are you and Larry happy?

SUE ANN
Oh, I dunno... enough, I s'pose.

BETTY
Then you should treasure that... you gotta hold on to whatever you got that's any good, even if it's only a little bit.

SUE ANN
All you been through... I ever tell you what a good friend you are?

BETTY
All the time...

SUE ANN
Well, you are.

After a beat...

BETTY
Something bad happened to Del and me, didn't it?

SUE ANN
Yeah, hon. Real bad. You just get some sleep, everything's gonna be fine.

BETTY
Sue Ann, I'm sorry about all this, but I just know there's something special out there for me...

Sue Ann looks down at her friend, troubled. She strokes Betty's hair gently and kisses her. After she leaves, Betty lies awake, staring at the ceiling. A mobile dangles overhead.

LATER

The Mickey Mouse clock on the wall reads 3:30. Beneath it, Betty is sitting up in bed, wide awake.

44 INT. SUE ANN'S HOUSE - LIVING ROOM - NIGHT 44

Betty comes down the stairs without a sound. She finds a pen and paper near the phone and writes a note.

INSERT: Dear Del:

This is the hardest thing I've ever done and I can't even face you. But I need to be honest. We haven't been happy for a long time. You always say people need their space, and now you'll have some. I'm sorry.

Betty

She takes off her wedding band and puts it on the table.

45 EXT. BETTY'S HOUSE/GARAGE - NIGHT 45

Betty raises the garage door, tosses her overnight bag and birthday money envelope into the LeSabre, and gets in.

She drives through Fair Oaks, past the town limits. She keeps on driving until her car recedes into the moonlit prairie horizon.

46 EXT./INT. LESABRE - DRIVING - NIGHT 46

She comes to a sudden halt in front of the "You are Leaving Kansas" billboard. She stares hard at it through the windshield. Suddenly, she hits the gas and bolts off along the Oklahoma blacktop. She never looks back.

47 INT. BETTY'S LESABRE - THE NEXT DAY 47

Betty yawns, looks at her watch and increases her speed. When she sees a sign for a MOTEL ahead, she pulls off the highway.

48 EXT. TRUCK STOP/MOTEL - DAY 48

She parks at a truck stop/restaurant/motel complex, hops out and runs to the motel office window.

49 INT. TRUCK STOP - MOTEL ROOM - DAY 49

Betty enters her room, immediately turns on the TV, and plops down on the bed.

VOICE (V.O.)
And now we return to "A Reason to Love."

50 EXT. TRUCK STOP/MOTEL PARKING LOT - SAME TIME 50

A crowded truck stop in the Texas flatlands. THREE TRUCK DRIVERS in jeans, flannel shirts and denim jackets walk across the parking lot.

One is an old, grizzled veteran with a salt-and-pepper stubble and a greasy CAT cap on his head. It's CHARLIE. Next to him is DUANE, a burly young driver in fancy cowboy boots. Flanking Duane is WESLEY.

WESLEY
So you got Asian women?

DUANE
(Southern accent)
Sure, I got Asian. Got black, white, any color you like, video and magazine. Got fat chicks and animals too, if you want 'em. They're extra...

CHARLIE
Mmmm. Well, it was a piece of luck running into you, Duane. I thought I was
(MORE)

CHARLIE (cont'd)
gonna have to take Wesley out and hose him down. All he talks about is those Japanese gals.

WESLEY
I like 'em small. When you're inside a little Asian chick, it's like your dick is the axle that holds her body together.

DUANE
That's nicely put. You outta get yourself to Thailand...

They reach Duane's truck, an empty car-carrier with Michigan plates, and climb up into the cab.

51 INT. DUANE'S TRUCK - DAY 51

Two Confederate flags criss-cross over Duane's CB unit. On the dashboard is a Rebel flag pin, a bumper sticker that says "The South Will Rise Again" and a dozen country music tapes.

Duane gets in the sleeper cab, where stacks of porno tapes and magazines reach the ceiling. Wesley takes the driver's seat, Charlie, the passenger seat.

CHARLIE
What part of Dixie are you from, Duane?

DUANE
Georgia. In case I didn't tell you, it's cash only, gentlemen.

WESLEY
We can live with that.

CHARLIE
I'm a Yankee, myself. Massachusetts.

Duane passes two videos to Wesley.

DUANE
Here's Ghengis Kunt and The Demilitarized Zone. Get it?
(laughs)
They're Korean, so they're pretty hot.

CHARLIE
You know, it's interesting. The South lost the Civil War, but they still seem to get all the glory.

DUANE
Huh?

CHARLIE
Jeb Stuart, Stonewall Jackson, Jefferson Davis - they're all losers in my book.

Charlie smiles. Duane stops digging through the videotapes.

DUANE
The fuck you talking about?

CHARLIE
Even Robert E. Lee was a loser.

DUANE
(to Wesley)
He goin' crazy on us, or what?

CHARLIE
Did you know the most brutal, inhumane prison of the entire war was in Georgia?

DUANE
Really. And where was that, old man?

CHARLIE
Andersonville.
(BEAT)
They did horrible things to men there...

52 INT. CHLOE'S APARTMENT - NIGHT - (ON TV SCREEN) 52

Chloe is curled up on her white leather sofa, cowering as Lonnie hovers over her accusingly.

LONNIE
I think you better tell me what's going on here, Chloe.

CHLOE
I just feel... funny about what we did.

LONNIE
(laughs)
You feel guilty? Let me remind you of something, sweetheart. You're in this up to those fabulous eyes of yours. Understand?

The camera holds on her face for a melodramatic beat ... Chloe's trapped, and she knows it.

PULL BACK to reveal Betty lying on the bed in her motel room, out cold.

53 INT. DUANE'S TRUCK - LATER 53

The flag poles over the CB unit are bare. Duane is in the sleeper cab, his forearms bound to his thighs with duct tape. A telltale piece of Confederate red fabric hangs out of his mouth. There is a purplish bruise on his forehead. He's quiet, but glowering at his captors.

CHARLIE
... So, at a rest stop outside Logansport you noticed that two guys were slipping something extra in one of your cars, and you decided to see what it was. Then you figured you'd take this valuable commodity and go into business yourself, even though it didn't belong to you. But you needed a crackerjack salesman to move it, so you made the biggest mistake of your short life and chose Del. Sound right so far?

Duane nods.

CHARLIE (cont'd)
Del's dead, by the way. I sent him to the Great Beyond.

WESLEY
Actually, I scalped him, and *then* you killed him.

Duane narrows his eyes in disbelief.

CHARLIE
Exactly.
(BEAT)
Now, the one thing I don't get is that we checked all the Buicks on that lot. Four '97 LeSabres and nothing in 'em.

Duane smiles mockingly.

CHARLIE
Ohhh ... There weren't four, were there?

Charlie reaches up above the visor and pulls down a rumpled manifest. He leafs through it.

CHARLIE (cont'd)
There were five, damn it! I should have known!! Goddamn...
(BEAT)
So, what happened to the fifth car?

Duane shrugs his shoulders.

CHARLIE
You know you're going to die, don't you, Duane?
(Duane nods)
And you really *don't* know where that other LeSabre is, do you?

Duane shakes his head. Charlie sighs, resigned.

CHARLIE (cont'd)
He's telling the truth. He doesn't know.

WESLEY
Should I kill him now?

CHARLIE
Wait. Any last words, General Lee?

Duane nods emphatically. Wesley pulls the Confederate flags out of his mouth.

DUANE
Suck my dick, you Yankee piece of shit.

He spits in Wesley's face. Charlie has to restrain Wesley.

CHARLIE
God, I admire that. Ya see that, Wesley? *That's* why they get all the glory.

Charlie climbs down from the big rig and heads across the parking lot. The Town Car is parked near the adjacent motel, just a few spaces away from Betty's LeSabre.

With a furious calm Wesley wipes his face, then takes out a can of lighter fluid, sets it on the dash and looks at Duane.

WESLEY
...why'd you spit on me?

54 EXT. TRUCK STOP/MOTEL PARKING LOT - DUSK 54

Charlie pulls the Town Car alongside Duane's rig and drums the steering wheel impatiently. It begins to rain. There are flashes of LIGHTNING in the distance.

CHARLIE
Come on, Wesley, three shots.

A FLASH OF ORANGE FLAME ignites inside Duane's cab. Charlie sighs. Finally, THREE DULL THUDS reverberate from inside. Wesley climbs down clutching a videotape and gets in the car.

CHARLIE (cont'd)
What the hell was that, another statement?

WESLEY
Well, no one ever spit in my face before. Especially some cracker fuck.

CHARLIE
You have to rise above it. The professionals rise above that kind of thing...

As they drive away FLAMES are beginning to dance inside the cab.

55 INT. TRUCK STOP/MOTEL ROOM - EVENING 55

The FLICKERING LIGHT of the TV screen is the only light. Betty lies asleep on the bed. The NEWS comes on and she starts to stir as ...

NEWSCASTER
... small town of Fair Oaks ... has left people shaken ... owner-manager of Sizemore Motors ...

Betty sits up. On the TV screen is a shot of Del as Julius Caesar from one of his commercials.

NEWSCASTER
(cont'd)
... police are still investigating.

She blinks at the screen, confused, as the next story comes on. Betty reaches for the phone.

56 INT. POLICE STATION - EVENING 56

Ballard is doing paperwork. Roy is asleep on a nearby bench. A DEPUTY picks up a ringing phone and hands it to Ballard.

DEPUTY
Sheriff, it's Betty Sizemore, on two!

BALLARD
SHHH!... (Whispering) BETTY? WHERE ARE YOU?

57 INT. TRUCK STOP/MOTEL ROOM - ON BETTY 57

BETTY
I'm in a motel. Has something happened to Del? Did he do something stupid?

BALLARD (V.O.)
BETTY, I NEED TO TALK TO YOU...IN PERSON! WHERE'RE YOU AT?

BETTY
IF THIS IS ABOUT DEL, FORGET IT! I'M NOT COMING BACK!

BALLARD (V.O.)
GODAMMIT, BETTY! ... WHO'S CHLOE?

BETTY
I'M THROUGH TALKING NOW! GOODBYE!

She hangs up. HEADLIGHTS sweep across the curtains, startling her.

58 INT. BETTY'S LESABRE - MOVING - DAY 58

Betty crosses the border from Texas into New Mexico. She grips the wheel intently, driving for all she's worth.

59 OMIT 59

60 EXT. FAIR OAKS TRAILER PARK - LATE AFTERNOON 60

Betty's blue Corsica sits surrounded by yellow police tape. Half a dozen COPS mill around. To one side are several REPORTERS and PHOTOGRAPHERS, Roy included. A FEW RESIDENTS mill around in the background.

A stack of pictures of Betty sit on a makeshift table.

REPORTER #1
Who witnessed Ms. Sizemore driving here?

BALLARD
The Assistant Manager, Mr. Wylie.

REPORTER #2
But he couldn't identify the male passenger?

BALLARD
Only to say he was wearing green.

ROY
What if the killers didn't see her? You published her picture - you're gonna get her killed!

BALLARD
No, we're bringing the community into the effort to find her.

ROY
You're lying!

BALLARD
I spoke to Betty Sizemore yesterday.
(the reporters hush)
That's right. There's no doubt in my mind, folks... she's on the run. Whether or not she's mixed up in all this remains to be seen...

ROY
That's bullshit, Sheriff! You think she's a suspect!

BALLARD
I'd like to apologize for our local boy. He's been in love with Betty since the fifth grade, y'see. He means well, but he's in over his head on this.

61 INT. TIP TOP DINER - NEXT MORNING 61

CLOSE SHOT of a headline in the *Wichita Eagle*: "EYE WITNESS TO BRUTAL MURDER MISSING" over a picture of Betty. Charlie is one of MANY CUSTOMERS reading a copy. Wesley is plowing through a stack of pancakes.

WESLEY
So how do we know that car's still in Fair Oaks?

CHARLIE
We don't. But a '97 Le Sabre'll be easy to find if it's here, town this size...
(BEAT)
He said he gave his wife some car as a gift, remember?

Charlie turns the page for emphasis and studies Betty's features.

CHARLIE (cont'd)
This is bad, Wesley. Very, very bad.

Wesley happily adds three strips of bacon brought by A WAITRESS, who wears a button with the word "Missing" over Betty's face.

CHARLIE (cont'd)
... extremely bad.

Wesley finally looks up, directly at the picture of Betty.

CHARLIE (cont'd)
Did you hear what I said?

Wesley nods, his mouth stuffed with food.

CHARLIE (cont'd)
Maybe you don't appreciate the gravity of this situation. It's bad enough that we don't have what we came here for. It's worse that we don't know where it is. And now *this*.
(points at the headline)
This was supposed to be my last job. I already put the deposit down on my boat.
(BEAT)
How can you eat at a time like this? I get nauseous just watching you...

WESLEY
I can eat because I know we didn't kidnap that woman. I can eat because they aren't looking for us. And I can eat 'cause I'm fucking *hungry*...
(off Charlie's look)
... relax. She's gonna end up on a milk carton and that's about it.

CHARLIE
I hope you're right...

WESLEY
... I know I am. Let's just do what we gotta do here, and get the fuck gone.

They sit for a moment in silence. Wesley swallowing without chewing and Charlie studying Betty's photo.

CHARLIE
She got out of town awfully fast. And wasn't she quiet in that house? I think most women would have screamed, don't you? I know they would've...
(BEAT)
(MORE)

CHARLIE (cont'd)
We could be dealing with a cunning, ruthless woman...

62 INT./EXT. SUE ANN'S HOUSE - DAY 62

Sue Ann opens her front door to find Wesley standing before her. It's a new Wesley: glasses, conservative suit, and a convincingly humble manner.

WESLEY
Mrs. Rogers? I'm Dwight Campbell, with Neighborly Life Insurance. I'm looking for Betty Sizemore.

SUE ANN
I wish I could help you, but I can't.

Wesley is hit by a flying action figure. He doesn't flinch. Kids run by.

WESLEY
Aren't they precious?
(BEAT)
Ma'am, she has a substantial death benefit coming to her from the tragic loss of her husband. Does she have any relatives in the area?

SUE ANN
No.
(BEAT)
Well, her grandparents are down in Oklahoma, but that's it...

WESLEY
I see. And are you in touch with Mrs. Sizemore?

SUE ANN
No. But I'm taping her show every day so she can watch it when she comes back.

WESLEY
Her show?

SUE ANN
"A Reason to Love."

Wesley's eyes light up. He can't help himself.

WESLEY
I see.
(BEAT)
Did Chloe testify?

SUE ANN
(reassuring)
I don't think she will. She's a slut, but I just don't think she's that mean. Jasmine'll bring her around...

WESLEY
Jasmine... Do you have yesterday's show on tape, by any chance?

Sue Ann holds the door open, smiling, and Wesley enters. .

63 INT. TIP TOP DINER - KANSAS - DAY 63

Charlie nurses a cup of coffee at the counter while talking to Darlene. His Federal Marshall's badge rests on the counter. Shehands him two photos of Betty taken at her birthday celebration. In one she's holding the cardboard David Ravell. The other, a closeup shot.

CHARLIE
... and how long did she work here?

DARLENE
Oh, five years, give or take.

CHARLIE
Hmm... you two in high school together?

DARLENE
Aren't you a sweetheart... no, not quite. Anyway, she's been with us awhile.

CHARLIE
But she wanted more out of life, right?

DARLENE
No... she just wanted *something* outta life. Anything. And with Del, she wasn't getting nothing. That's her husband, Del. I'm sorry about what happened and all, but that's the way I feel about all of this...

CHARLIE
I see.
(holding up photos)
May I?

DARLENE
If it helps bring her back, be my guest...

CHARLIE
Thank you for your cooperation.
(BEAT)
Just one more thing... did she ever talk about getting rich?

DARLENE
... who doesn't?

Darlene tries to smile and returns to the kitchen. Charlie studies the snapshots, comparing them.

64 INT. APARTMENT/BEDROOM - DAY 64

Wesley is in bed on top of Joyce, humping her slowly.

WESLEY
... and what kind of car does she drive?

JOYCE
Well, she wanted a LeSabre, but Del made her use that blue Corsica...
(BEAT)
So, is this what you boys'd call 'pumping me for information?'

Joyce GIGGLES as Wesley stops moving.

WESLEY
Did you say LeSabre?

JOYCE
Look, she didn't kill Del over no car if that's what you're thinking.

WESLEY
But she could have taken one, right?

With her knees, Joyce prods him into humping her again.

JOYCE
Maybe, but I don't think she had the nerve. I know her. And I'm a pretty good judge of character...

Joyce reaches for a cigarette on the nightstand and takes a deep drag. Wesley closes his eyes and turns away, offended.

WESLEY
... yeah, I can see that.

65 EXT. DESERT ROAD - WILLIAMS, ARIZONA - DAY 65

Betty drives along a lonely stretch of highway that slowly reveals a desert town in the distance.

66 INT. CANYON RANCH BAR - DAY 66

Big ol' place. Lots of wood and red leather. Betty rushes in as the clock on the wall reads 2:58. The Town Drunk, MERLE, is alone at the bar watching "Bass Masters" on a huge TV screen. In front of him is a remote control. A FEW OTHERS at tables.

Betty sidles up to the bar and sits down. She looks at Merle, at the clock, at the remote.

BETTY
Would you mind very much if I changed the channel at three o'clock?

MERLE
Yes.

He BURPS, then finally looks at her with bleary eyes.

BETTY
Please? It's very important to me. "A Reason to Love" comes on at three around here.

He ignores her. Betty puts her wallet on the bar.

BETTY (cont'd)
I'll give you money.

Merle SLAMS his hand down on the bar, scaring her.

MERLE
ARE YOU DEAF?!!

It's 3:01. ELLEN DRABER, 40's, appears behind the bar, looks at the clock and takes the remote from Merle. She changes the channel to "A Reason to Love" as the opening titles end.

Betty can't believe it. Merle smiles at her wickedly.

MERLE (cont'd)
Please keep it down, it's time for "A Reason to Love..."

BETTY
That's real funny. Why don't you have another drink?

ELLEN
What's the matter here?

BETTY
I _begged_ him to let me put that on!

ELLEN
He's a prick. Merle?... You're a prick.

MERLE grunts in reply. Ellen turns back to Betty.

ELLEN
So you're into "Reason," too? Finally, someone civilized! I'm Ellen, what can I get you?

BETTY
Hi, I'm Betty. I'll take a Miller, if you got it...

67 INT. CHLOE'S APARTMENT - DAY (ON TV SCREEN) 67

Chloe paces in front of her white sofa, a matching white telephone in her hand. She looks worried.

ELLEN (O.S.)
What's that bitch up to now?

We hear the BEEP TONE of an answering machine.

CHLOE
Lonnie? It's Chloe. We need to talk ... I don't think I can go through with this.

She hangs up. The camera stays on her for a melodramatic beat of introspection as we GO TO COMMERCIAL.

68 INT. CANYON RANCH BAR - RETURN TO BAR 68

BETTY
Do you have a phone?

Ellen swings a phone up onto the bar.

ELLEN
If it's long distance you can leave me a buck when you're done.

Betty dials ...

BETTY
Sue Ann? It's Betty. I just wanted to let you know I'm okay ... Huh? I'm at the Canyon Ranch Bar in ...
(looks at Ellen)

MERLE
Phoenix...

ELLEN
Shut up, Merle... Williams.

BETTY
Williams, Arizona. About halfway there, I guess.

69 INT. SUE ANN'S HOUSE - DAY 69

Sue Ann is in her kitchen, ignoring the pleas of all three children.

SUE ANN
Halfway *where*? You've gotta come home. We've been worried sick about you. Are you alright?

BETTY (V.O.)
Sue Ann, I thought you of all people would back me up on this, you know what Del's like. How did he take my note?

SUE ANN
Betty, honey, listen to me. A man came by from Mutual Life Insurance. He says you've got money comin' to you from Del's policy.
(BEAT)
Del's *life* insurance policy-- Are you with me?

BETTY (V.O.)
What are you talking about?

70 INT. CANYON RANCH BAR - DAY 70

"A REASON TO LOVE" comes back on the TV.

BETTY
Tell Del I'm sorry. I left so quick, but I need to do this.

SUE ANN (V.O.)
Do what?

BETTY
I gotta go.

SUE ANN (V.O.)
Betty! Listen to me! Del is ...

Betty hangs up.

71 INT. COCKTAIL LOUNGE - NIGHT (ON TV SCREEN) 71

David is at a bar staring into his drink. Lonnie is with him.

LONNIE
How you holding up, amigo?

DAVID
I just wish I knew why she's doing it.

LONNIE
Yeah. Women are an unsolved mystery.

ELLEN (O.S.)
If that little weasel ever walked in here
I wouldn't serve him.

BETTY (O.S.)
I'd slap his face.

ELLEN (O.S.)
I'd kick him in the nuts, if I thought he
had any.

DISSOLVE TO:

72 INT. CANYON RANCH BAR - LATER 72

There are two empty beer bottles in front of Betty. The THEME MUSIC and CLOSING CREDITS of "A Reason to Love" are playing. Betty pushes the phone back across the bar.

ELLEN
Where you headed, Betty?

BETTY
Los Angeles, California.

ELLEN
And you called your friend, and she's
telling you not to go?
(Betty nods)
When I went to Europe my friends told me
I was crazy.

BETTY
Europe? *The* Europe?
(laughs)
This is my first time out of Kansas.

ELLEN
I should call you Dorothy.
(BEAT)
When I left here I went straight to Italy. Everybody told me not to go. But I wanted to go to Rome ever since I saw Audrey Hepburn in "Roman Holiday," and goddamnit, I went.

BETTY
Did you love it?

ELLEN
Sure I loved it! It was great.

Ellen rinses a few glasses as she talks to Betty.

ELLEN
Let me tell you something. I got groped by these Tunisian guys who thought I was a slut for wearing shorts, it was hotter than stink the whole time, and I got some kind of weird gum disease from the water. Plus, it ended my marriage--

BETTY
That's horrible!

ELLEN
No, he was a toad. Even more of a toad than Merle... I just wear the ring to keep the flies away. Rome was the best thing I ever did, because I DID IT! And I swear to you, it changed me. I've been to Rome, Italy! I sat every morning at the Cafe Sistina and had my cappuccino, and watched the pilgrims walk to mass, and no one can ever take that away from me.

Betty leans across the bar conspiratorially. She looks at Merle to make sure he won't hear her.

BETTY
I left my husband two days ago.

ELLEN
Really?

BETTY
I'm getting back with my ex-fiancé. He proposed to me right around here, so I guess this is just sort of a sentimental stop...

ELLEN
Wait, I thought you said you'd never been outta Kansas...

BETTY
Oh. I mean, except for that.
(BEAT)
Yep. I'm trading in a car dealer for a heart specialist, so that's pretty good...

ELLEN
Nice move. Cedars Sinai?

BETTY
No. Loma Vista.

ELLEN
(laughs)
I s'pose his name's David Ravell.

BETTY
(truly shocked)
How did you know?

ELLEN
What's his real name?

BETTY
Dr. David Ravell.

ELLEN
You mean... George McCord, the actor?

BETTY
No, I mean David Ravell. He's a surgeon.

Ellen looks at Betty.

ELLEN
Yeah, I know, we just watched him together, remember? Up there on the TV.
(off Betty's earnest look)
Good God Almighty ... You're serious. I've heard about people like you.

Ellen whistles, wipes the bar down to buy a few seconds. Merle looks over at Betty, then catches Ellen's eye.

ELLEN
Piss off, Merle.
(to Betty)
So how you gonna find him, Betty?

BETTY
I'll go to the Hospital.

ELLEN
What if you *can't* find him? What if you get out there, and *nothing's* the way you thought it was gonna be?

BETTY
Like Rome?

ELLEN
Worse.

BETTY
You made out alright.

ELLEN
Yeah, but at least I knew Rome was gonna be there when I arrived...

Ellen walks to the end of the bar and starts rinsing glasses. After a beat, Betty gets up and moves down close to her.

BETTY
Ellen, this is the biggest thing I've ever done, but I've gotta do it.

ELLEN
You take care of yourself then, Betty, and don't let anybody stop you...

BETTY
To tell you the truth, I can't believe I've made it this far. It may not be Europe, but I just know there's something special out there for me...

Ellen looks into Betty's eyes - sees the innocence, the hope and enthusiasm - and has to look away. Betty takes it as her cue to leave. She smiles, puts two dollars on the bar near the phone and leaves. Ellen stands perfectly still, watching the door.

MERLE
What planet is *she* from?

73 INT. BETTY'S LESABRE - GRAND CANYON - MOVING - DAY 73

Betty approaches the GRAND CANYON, driving slowly along the South Rim, searching for a specific spot. Finally, she pulls over abruptly. This is it. We can tell by the joy in her expression.

74 EXT. GRAND CANYON - DAY 74

Betty walks to the rail and gazes out at the canyon. Turning her head slowly, as if expecting it, she sees DAVID RAVELL leaning on the rail about twenty feet away, clutching a bouquet of roses.

Betty starts toward him... he starts toward her... A magic moment... Shattered when a black sedan appears, inching its way along. She freezes. David vanishes, and ...

An ELDERLY MAN helps his wife out of the car and snaps her picture in front of the canyon. Betty moves away.

75 INT. LINCOLN TOWN CAR - KANSAS - MOVING - NIGHT 75

Charlie and Wesley drive across Kansas farm country.

CHARLIE
So she gets rid of the asshole and is set for life in the same day.

WESLEY
You think so? Joyce says she's timid.

CHARLIE
Joyce was screwing Del.

WESLEY
... among others.

CHARLIE
I'd say that about torches her credibility, wouldn't you?

WESLEY
Yeah, well, if the wife's trying to sell it she'll fuck up. She's an amateur, just like Del was.

The CAR PHONE RINGS. Charlie answers.

CHARLIE
Maybe...
(into phone)
Yes?

SUE ANN (V.O.)
Is this Neighborly Life Insurance?

CHARLIE
Sorry, you've got the wrong number.

He hangs up.

CHARLIE
No, I see Betty as a Midwestern Stoic type. Ice water in her veins. A clear thinker. Probably a Swede or a Finn.

WESLEY
A 'Finn?' What is a Finn?

CHARLIE
You should read more. Listen to me. I think this woman was waiting for a chance to do this, and we gave it to her. She kept to herself for years, living with a pompous asshole. Then she sees her opportunity, and BOOM! - she leaves that little mudpatch in the dust. These heartlanders can't figure it out, 'cause that's not their sweet little Betty. Hah! We've been tracking her for, what, three days and I already understand her better'n most the people in that shitty little burg.

Charlie pulls out the close-up photo and studies it.

CHARLIE (cont'd)
Betty, Betty, Betty...

WESLEY
So what the fuck's a Finn?

CHARLIE
Oh, for Chrissakes. It just means the kind of person who can eat shit for a long time without complaining, then cut their momma's throat and go dancing the same night.

WESLEY
Like... us?

CHARLIE
No,... like a worthy adversary, Wesley. Like a very worthy adversary.

76 OMIT 76

76A INT. ROY'S APARTMENT - DAY 76A

Roy approaches his fish tank cautiously. He leans down and looks at the piranha as a TV commercial ends and "A Reason to Love" comes on.

He then returns to his computer, struggling to find the right words and to type them with only one hand. He types a little, stares at the screen, then deletes an entire sentence one character at a time, hammering on the 'Delete' key. He glances up at the television as the words 'Chloe' and 'Lonnie' are repeated.

77 INT. POLICE STATION - BALLARD'S OFFICE - THE NEXT DAY 77

Roy and Sue Ann go straight to Ballard's office, where they find him at his desk eating lunch out of tupperware containers. He wears a napkin tucked into his shirt-top.

BALLARD
What the hell do *you* want?... Hey, Sue Ann, what's up?

ROY
We think we know where Betty is.

BALLARD
Ah, shit... Do I have to hear this *now*?

SUE ANN
What's with the tupperware, Elden, did Meredith run outta baggies?

BALLARD
No reason to get a plate dirty.

ROY
I see you're sticking to the diet Betty put you on...

BALLARD
Worry about your own goddamn lunch!

ROY
(excited; to Sue Ann)
Tell him what you told me.

SUE ANN
Betty is a big, big fan of the soap opera, "A Reason to Love." Look...

She tosses a copy of "Soap Opera Digest" on the desk. Ballard ignores it and keeps eating.

BALLARD
Why do I need to see this? Did he ask you to...?

ROY
Listen! I saw 'Chloe' and 'Lonnie' on T.V. They're television characters.

SUE ANN
Betty's in love with Dr. David Ravell, from the show. What if she's out in Los Angeles looking for him? The actor, I mean...

BALLARD
That's the dumbest thing I've ever heard.

ROY
Yeah? Well, she called Sue Ann yesterday from Arizona.

BALLARD
She said she was in Arizona, did she?

ROY & SUE ANN
Yes!!

BALLARD
You people are even more stupid than I thought. The woman's on the run and she's gonna just phone in her location?

SUE ANN
Come on, Elden, she's not on the run. Couldn't you at least call the Los Angeles Police Department?

ROY
You *gotta* do that much.

BALLARD
Hey, I'm the law. I don't *gotta* do nothing...

78 EXT. FARMHOUSE - OKLAHOMA - DAY 78

The Lincoln pulls into the dusty, overgrown driveway and front yard of a derelict farm.

79 INT. FARMHOUSE / KITCHEN - DAY 79

The remains of pie and coffee on the table, Charlie and Wesley kick back with JERROLD BLAINE and his wife ELIZABETH, both in their 80's. Photos of Betty at various ages lie scattered in front of them.

Charlie holds up a picture of a young Betty in ballerina costume posing at the barre. He studies it intently.

ELIZABETH
This is Betty at twelve.

CHARLIE
Very graceful. Perfect form.

ELIZABETH
Betty was a lovely child.

JERROLD
And she always had such spirit! But, after her mother died...

WESLEY
Would you say she was ambitious?

JERROLD
Oh, there's no tellin' what that girl could've accomplished, and she never had it easy. Never really had a childhood... caring for her father, going to school.

Charlie admires a photo of Betty, around 18 years old. He continues to rummage through a box of collectibles, pocketing a small child's diary when it is convenient.

CHARLIE
Wise beyond her years, I'm sure, and such poise, too.
(quietly)
Very, very impressive...

WESLEY
Well, then, did you ever get any indication that she wanted to leave her husband?

ELIZABETH
I don't like talking bad about the dead, but now that he's gone I can tell you she put up with things in that marriage I wouldn't have. And yes, she, of all people, was the one who defended him. And that's why what that sheriff said makes me so angry.

CHARLIE
What do you mean?

ELIZABETH
If anyone had paid to have that husband of hers killed, it would have been me.

CHARLIE
(taking her hand)
Mrs. Blaine? I can tell you right now, without a doubt, that your granddaughter is alive, and did not kill Del Sizemore.

JERROLD
You've got to be missing a piece of your soul to kill someone. That's not our Betty...

WESLEY
(defensive)
... why do you think you have to be missing a piece of your soul to kill somebody?

JERROLD
Because it ain't natural, young man.

WESLEY
What are you talking about? Killing's totally natural. It's dying that isn't natural...

CHARLIE
(covering)
My partner's still young, Mr. Blaine, and he loves his job.
(laughs)
He'd like to kill all the criminals himself!
(BEAT)
Now, if Betty was running from someone, where do you think she'd go?

80-82 OMIT 80-82

83 INT. BETTY'S LESABRE/ EXT. COUNTY USC HOSPITAL - MOVING - AFTERNOON 83

Betty drives through Boyle Heights - East L.A., holding a map and checking street signs. She is wearing a brand new Nurse's uniform. Up ahead, she sees the hillside complex of L.A. County/USC Hospital. Hurriedly, she pulls over and checks herself in the visor mirror. She is underwhelmed.

BETTY
God... I still look like a waitress.

84 INT. HOSPITAL - CHIEF NURSE'S OFFICE - AFTERNOON 84

The CHIEF NURSE, a large, dynamic woman in her 50's, faces Betty across her desk.

CHIEF NURSE
Of course, I don't know *every* doctor who works here...

BETTY
Dr. Ravell's the finest surgeon on the staff. You must know him. He's incredibly handsome, gentle, considerate. He's being sued for sexual assault right now, but--
(Off Chief Nurse's look)
It's not true. He was set up.

CHIEF NURSE
Well, I certainly would have heard about that.

BETTY
Of course, he's only here two days a week. He's also on staff over at Loma Vista.

CHIEF NURSE
... I don't think I know that hospital.

BETTY
It's in a very pretty area that gets a lot of sun, has palm trees out front, mountains in the background...

CHIEF NURSE
Really? You've just described all of Southern California.

The Chief Nurse looks at Betty for a moment, then stands abruptly, signaling the end of the interview.

CHIEF NURSE
(cont'd)
Well, I'm sorry, but I can't even consider you without references or a resume. And frankly, I don't know how you could have forgotten them.

85 INT. HOSPITAL / HALLWAY - LATER 85

On her way down the hall Betty passes a patient's room when the sound of A PERSON MOANING stops her. She can't help but go inside. A TV plays commercials.

AN OLDER WOMAN lies in bed, alone and staring at the ceiling. Betty looks around and notices several arrangements of flowers on a deserted nightstand. She brings them over to the older woman's bedside, positions them, then gently strokes her head.

BETTY
There... you rest now.

The woman's eyes flutter. She is disoriented at first, then calms as she adjusts to the comforting sight of Betty. Betty takes her hand.

OLDER WOMAN
Who... who're you?

BETTY
I'm... I'm Nurse Betty.

The woman smiles serenely at this and begins to drift off. Betty checks her monitors as the opening credits of "A Reason to Love" begin to play.

She glances up at the doorway at the same moment and sees Dr. David Ravell standing at the entrance. He checks the chart on the door, smiles warmly at Betty and then moves off. In a flash, Betty is up and after him.

The THEME MUSIC is her private soundtrack as she checks out every man in surgical scrubs, looking for David Ravell.

Then... She sees him. In all his glory at the end of a corridor walking away from her. Betty gives chase. She gains steadily on him, her heart racing. As they near Emergency the NOISE LEVEL picks up.

He stops at the nurses' station. Betty closes the gap. She starts to run.

BETTY
DAVID!!!

He turns to face her ... It's not David Ravell.

BETTY (cont'd)
Sorry, I thought you were someone else.
(BEAT)
Do you know Dr. David Ravell?

The man shakes his head. Betty keeps going, looking around: it's incredible - the size, the activity, the intensity.

86 INT. HOSPITAL - EMERGENCY AREA - SAME TIME 86

DOZENS OF PATIENTS lie on gurneys awaiting treatment in a holding area. It's still more intense at the entrance: VOICES talking back and forth urgently, POLICE OFFICERS, CIVILIANS, DOCTORS AND NURSES converging.

87 EXT. HOSPITAL - EMERGENCY AREA - LATE AFTERNOON 87

FIVE AMBULANCES unload patients at the same time. At that moment a group of TWENTY JAPANESE HOSPITAL ADMINISTRATORS reaches the E.R. portion of their tour.

A WHITE MERCEDES tears up the ramp and SCREECHES to a stop. A YOUNG MAN in gang colors is pushed out, bleeding heavily. A DOCTOR runs at the Mercedes to head it off, yelling indignantly. The car plows right into him and takes off.

Another ambulance crests the ramp, lights flashing. The Mercedes SLAMS into it head-on. NURSES AND DOCTORS run into the parking lot. A GANGBANGER gets out of the Mercedes, dazed and wobbly. He pulls a pistol. Everyone dives for cover.

The Mercedes driver is unconscious. The driver of the smashed up ambulance is slumped over the wheel. The rear doors fly open, and a young Hispanic woman, ROSA HERRERA, leaps out.

ROSA
SOMEBODY HELP US! PLEASE, SOMEBODY!

Doctors and nurses work on patients and try to get to the injured doctor, but the kid with the gun keeps them away. SECURITY GUARDS draw their guns and scream at him to drop it.

ROSA (cont'd)
WHY ISN'T ANYBODY HELPING US?!!
(to gunman in Spanish)
Hey, you little shit! If I had a gun I'd shoot you right now!

The loading area is jammed with panicked people. Doctors and nurses creep out of the hospital on all fours, trying to stay low. No one is getting to Rosa, whose frantic eyes find Betty. They look right at each other.

ROSA (cont'd)
What are you standing there for?!

Betty walks toward her calmly, indifferent to the danger as Rosa pulls the gurney out of the ambulance herself. A PARAMEDIC lies unconscious inside.

ROSA (cont'd)
You gotta help him, he's hurt bad!!

On the gurney is a YOUNG MAN with a chest wound, nearly dead from blood loss. A DOCTOR appears and quickly examines him while keeping one eye on the gunman. He looks up at Betty.

DOCTOR #1
Forget it! He doesn't have a chance. Help us over here.

The doctor takes off. Rosa looks at Betty, crying.

ROSA
Please!

Betty hesitates, then checks his pulse - he has none. She peels back the bandages over a huge chest wound.

ROSA
Danny, it's gonna be all right!

Betty looks at Rosa again; looks around for help - there's no one. She plunges her fingers into the wound.

ROSA (cont'd)
(panic)
What are you doing?

BETTY
He has no heartbeat!

ROSA
You're hurting him!!

BETTY
I'm massaging his heart. I saw it done once.

ROSA
ARE YOU CRAZY?!! STOP IT!!!

BETTY
LISTEN TO ME! IF I DON'T DO THIS, HE'S DEAD!

She keeps working on him. We hear a GUNSHOT, and the kid with the pistol falls to the pavement. The loading area immediately fills with DOCTORS, NURSES and COPS.

BETTY
All right, we're moving him inside! Give me a hand!

Rosa is shocked into motion. Together they wheel Danny toward the entrance. A DOCTOR and TWO NURSES come out to take over. Betty, her white uniform now covered in blood, steps aside.

88 INT. HOSPITAL - EMERGENCY ROOM - LATER 88

The DOCTOR tries to calm Rosa and keep her from entering the treatment area.

ROSA
Is he gonna live?

DOCTOR
He's got a chance. Thanks to what that nurse did.

They exit together as AN ADMINISTRATOR and several Japanese officials approach. The Chief Nurse hovers nearby.

ADMINISTRATOR
(to Chief Nurse)
Harriet? Who is that remarkable nurse?

CHIEF NURSE
That's Betty Sagamore. I hired her today.

89 INT. CHEAP HOTEL - NIGHT 89

SEVERAL LOW LIFES are hanging out in the lobby. When Betty comes in with a bag of groceries they look up, ready to hassle her as she approaches the DESK CLERK.

BETTY
May I have my key, please?

She puts the bag on the counter, revealing that the front of her white uniform is covered with blood. She smiles at the low lifes, stopping them in their tracks.

90 INT./EXT. MOTEL ROOM - HOUSTON, TEXAS - DAY 90

The Town Car's looking a little muddy around the rims. Charlie and Wesley look tired as they wait in a seedy motel room. Charlie sits near a window, reading diary entries aloud. Wesley kicks back on the bed, fast-forwarding through "Genghis Kunt" and talking back to the screen.

WESLEY
Thas' it, thas' it... *conquer* that bitch.
(BEAT)
What time're they coming?

CHARLIE
It's not an exact science, Wesley. He said they'll be here... My Houston contact has always been very reliable.

WESLEY
And then we're gonna do her right here. Right?

CHARLIE
You're always so coarse... "Do her right here." Let's just see what happens, okay?
(reading)
"I wish that I could find a way; To speak my thoughts on Mother's Day. There are no words that quite express; My gratitude or happiness. A pleasant smile perhaps a kiss; I would not fail to give her this. I'd make her glad the whole day through; By sayin' 'Mother', I love you!' P.S. I wish I could say this to my mother's face, but I can't anymore."

Wesley rolls his eyes and turns up the volume. Finally a car pulls up outside and Charlie snaps the book closed. He makes a quick attempt to arrange himself and motions to Wesley, who turns off the tape.

A WOMAN with greasy blonde hair and skinny legs shown off by a short skirt comes in with another MAN. Charlie looks her over disgustedly as his face falls.

CHARLIE (cont'd)
Who are you?!
(to the man)
What the... Who the hell is this?

MAN #1
Easy, Charlie! She's exactly who you said you were looking for.

CHARLIE
Wait, wait a minute. We have a major miscommunication here. This not Betty. This is not even close to Betty...

WOMAN
What the fuck're you talking about? My name's Betty...

CHARLIE
Then I'm sorry... Wrong Betty.

WESLEY
Let's get out of here. We got another long drive ahead of us.
(BEAT)
... the fuck where I do not know, but I know it's gonna be long.

CHARLIE
(gathering his things)
Betty would never dress like that. She's not some trailer park slut!

WOMAN
Fuck you!

CHARLIE
And she doesn't have a sewer for a mouth...

WESLEY
Okay, thank you, goodbye... Keep in touch...

CHARLIE
... She's got class, and poise. Lots of poise...

The man looks at Charlie, then at Wesley, who shrugs in reply as he steers them out the door.

WESLEY
Will you ease off on the 'poise' shit, you're spooking me here...

91 INT. HOSPITAL - CHIEF NURSE'S OFFICE - DAY 91

The Chief Nurse sits behind her desk. Betty faces her like a student in the principal's office, now dressed in her white waitress uniform. She hopes no one notices.

CHIEF NURSE
What you did yesterday was reckless at best. You are not an employee of this hospital! If that boy dies I don't even want to think of the lawsuit that'll follow. Are we communicating here?

BETTY
Yes, ma'am.

CHIEF NURSE
Good. I'm prepared to offer you a job. You can help out in the pharmacy until your California certification and references arrive, but you are not to touch anyone. Is that totally clear?
(Betty nods)
Fine...

The Chief Nurse gets up, and Betty follows suit.

CHIEF NURSE
(cont'd)
You can start tomorrow. And don't say a word about this to anyone.
(studying Betty's uniform)
Is that issue?

BETTY
Umm... yes. Back home.

CHIEF NURSE
Alright. Oh, and one more thing about what you did yesterday... Well done.

92 INT. HOSPITAL - INTENSIVE CARE UNIT - DAY 92

Danny Herrera is in bed unconscious. Rosa and her MOTHER are keeping vigil when Betty enters. Rosa jumps to her feet.

ROSA
Hey, it's Supernurse! Betty, right?

Rosa hugs her and tells her mother in Spanish who Betty is.

ROSA (cont'd)
My mother doesn't speak English.

Sra. Herrera smiles at Betty and starts to cry. As she steps forward, Rosa stands aside. The short, stocky woman envelops Betty in a bearhug.

MOTHER
No podremos olvidar lo que hizo ayer.

ROSA
(translating)
We can't forget what you did yesterday ... How can my family ever repay you?

BETTY
Tell her I was just--

MOTHER
Yo sé que es su empleo, pero...

ROSA
She doesn't care if it was just your job... Danny would be dead now but for you.

Sra. Herrera kisses Betty's hands and smiles through her tears. Then she motions to Rosa to take her place as she goes to Danny's bedside. Betty picks up Danny's chart and reads it.

ROSA (cont'd)
You don't sound like you're from here.

BETTY
I'm not. I just drove in from Kansas.

ROSA
So why'd you come to L.A.?

BETTY
I came for love. My fiancé is here.

MOTHER
Bravo! Mi hija no hace nada para amor...

ROSA
You're making me look bad... My mother says I wouldn't move across the street for love.

BETTY
It's something I *had* to do. For David.

ROSA
'David.' That's your guy. So, you staying with him?

THE ICU NURSE enters and adjusts the bank of machines feeding, medicating and monitoring Danny. Betty watches with interest.

BETTY
No... I don't really know where he is yet. I'm at a hotel around the corner.

ROSA
Man, that is love.

MOTHER
Ella debe quedar contigo.

ROSA
What? Ahh, Mom says you should stay with me... Okay, yeah, why not?

Betty looks at Sra. Herrera curiously.

ROSA
You can go get your stuff right now. I'll walk you down.

BETTY
No, that's not, I couldn't...

ROSA
Listen, when someone does the kind of thing you did, you gotta do something in return. So, you stay with me until you find your David and live happily ever after. Okay?

Rosa follows Betty out the door.

93 EXT. ROSA'S APARTMENT - NIGHT 93

Betty and Rosa make their way up the stairs of a Silverlake apartment house.

At the sound of SCREECHING TIRES they both look down as a black Lincoln Town Car drives by. Betty shudders.

ROSA
You okay? This neighborhood, you get used to it...

She nods. Rosa continues to talk as they climb the many stairs that lead to her door.

ROSA (cont'd)
I got this apartment with a guy.

BETTY
The one you were telling me about?

ROSA
No, this one was worse...I had to have the place sprayed when he left. Twice... He was two guys before the last one--not counting a little office thing in there, which I'm trusting you with, 'cause if it gets out, I'm on the street...

94 INT. ROSA'S APARTMENT - SAME TIME 94

The place is neat. As well furnished as a legal assistant's salary will allow. The living room is dominated by a large glass tank filled with tropical fish. Betty checks out the space.

BETTY
It's lovely...I really like your aquarium.

ROSA
Yeah, well, at least fish don't use your razor or pee on the seat...

BETTY
Hmmm. Sounds like you've had a pretty tough go of it with men...

ROSA
Oh, I dunno...but just once I wish I'd run into a guy who noticed the Koi before my tits.

Betty smiles, a little embarrassed.

ROSA (cont'd)
...come on, I'll show you your room.

95 EXT. TEXAS HIGHWAY - THE NEXT DAY 95

The black Lincoln Town Car is parked on a lonely stretch of prairie highway. Wesley sits in the passenger seat with the door open. The RADIO is on. Charlie is on his cell phone nearby.

CHARLIE
(into phone)
No, we don't know where she is... I understand... No, we'll find her...
(BEAT)
I understand.

He hangs up and looks out at the horizon, where huge black storm clouds are gathering. Then he walks slowly to the hood of the car, staring at the ground in front of his feet.

WESLEY
What'd they say? Can we go back to Detroit?

Charlie rests his hands gently on the hood, as if considering buying the car. Wesley's MUSIC BANGS from the radio.

CHARLIE
They said find it. Find her, find it. Finish the job you were paid to do.

WESLEY
Half.

CHARLIE
What?

WESLEY
They paid us half. They still owe us half...

CHARLIE
(disappointed)
There it is again. That lousy attitude that got us here in the first place. That "make a statement," do an end zone dance, shake your ass and sue everybody in sight attitude that's dragging this whole country down the drain.
(BEAT)
They don't owe us shit, Wesley! WHEN YOU FINISH THE JOB, YOU GET PAID!! WE HAVEN'T FINISHED THE GODDAMN JOB!!

Charlie POUNDS on the hood of the car, scaring Wesley.

CHARLIE (cont'd)
That woman could be in any one of four states. Four big states where the deer and the antelope play, Wesley! We're not in *Rhode Island*!

WESLEY
I know that.

CHARLIE
AND TURN THAT FUCKING MUSIC OFF!

Wesley switches it off. Charlie turns his back to the car and addresses the angry clouds on the horizon.

CHARLIE (cont'd)
Do I deserve this? In the twilight of my career, do I deserve this? I don't think so! I've always tried to do what's right. I never took out anybody who didn't have it coming. I'm a professional!
(BEAT)
AND WHERE THE FUCK AM I? I'M IN PURGATORY!

WESLEY
Worse... you're in Texas.

CHARLIE
Well, I should be in FLORIDA now! If Carl hadn't gone in to get those stones removed, you wouldn't be here and I'd be on my way to the Keys. On my boat, RELAXING WITH A GLASS OF PORT!! Re-ti-red!

The first raindrops begin to fall.

CHARLIE (cont'd)
I'm very tired, Wesley! I've worked hard, and the work should be over, but IT'S NOT! This job is just beginning.
(he turns around)
GET IN THE CAR!

Wesley *is* in the car, but he's too scared to tell Charlie, whose eyes are blazing. Charlie silently walks around to the driver's side and gets in. He and Wesley stare at each other over a photo of Betty, which is between them on the dash.

Charlie starts the engine and snatches up the picture.

CHARLIE (cont'd)
What're you thinking, girl? What's going on in that pretty little mind of yours? Huh? You can tell me...

He paws at the picture, imploringly. He mutters to himself. Wesley shakes his head and stares out.

96 INT. HOSPITAL - PHARMACY - DAY 96

Betty sits in an office along with a CLERK who taps away at a computer keyboard while she studies a printed list of names.

BETTY
I can't find Loma Vista Hospital...

CLERK
I never *heard* of Loma Vista Hospital.

BETTY
I don't believe this! You're the second person here who's told me that. That's like Ford saying they never heard of GM!

CLERK
Try another county...

He exits.

97 INT. LAW FIRM - LATER 97

Rosa is on the phone at her desk in a law office.

BETTY (V.O.)
Hey, Rosa...it's Betty. How do you get to this town called 'Tustin?' It's in Orange County...

ROSA
Tustin? Take the Hollywood Freeway to the Five...

BETTY (V.O.)
The Five?

ROSA
Just look for the really crowded road and follow that.

BETTY (V.O.)
Okay...oh, umm, would you mind if I borrowed some clothes?

ROSA
Huh? Sure, look in my closet, take any dress you want!
(BEAT)
We're still on for tonight, right?

98 INT. EXAMINING ROOM - LATER 98

Betty stands in a sexy pink dress, trying to decide if she should put on a hospital gown and waits, tensing each time she hears a voice from the hallway. Finally, the DOORKNOB BEGINS TO TURN.

A man's hand and the bottom of a white sleeve appear. The door swings open and a silver-haired, bespectacled DOCTOR in his mid-60's enters. The nametag on his white coat reads "DAVID RAVELL, M.D."

99 INT. NIGHTCLUB - NIGHT 99

Tasteful jazz, plenty of red leather booths. Betty winds her way through a PACKED CROWD, passing out small white cards. Rosa spots her and goes over to meet her.

ROSA
You made it! Hey, that looks great on you. 'S classy... (BEAT) So, how'd it go today? You find him?

BETTY
Ummm...no, no. Different 'Ravell.'

Rosa starts to lead her to the bar.

BETTY (cont'd)
You know, the more I think about it, this really isn't David's kind of place.

ROSA
What are you talking about? This bar is packed with professional people!
(BEAT)
Everybody says if you're going to get married, this is the spot to meet someone... Luckily, I'm currently off men, so I've got the luxury of not giving a shit.

BETTY
I know what you mean, I recently had some trouble with a man, a different man...and David's still getting over Leslie.
(off Rosa's look)
His wife.

ROSA
He has a wife?!

BETTY
Had. She died in a car accident last year. She was decapitated.

ROSA
God, that's awful!

BETTY
It may not have been an accident. They never did find her head...

ROSA
Her 'head'?! You're making this up...

BETTY
No, no! Well, see, she was having an affair with a Russian diplomat who I believe was mixed up with the Mafia...

ROSA
Jesus, I thought my love life was crazy...

LATER

Rosa and Betty are sitting in a booth, talking over drinks. The place is a little quieter now.

ROSA (cont'd)
... so, we'll hit the library first and fan out from there. They've got all the L.A. phone books, plus medical directories...
(BEAT)
We're not gonna let him hide from you any more, okay? I'm making this my personal mission.

BETTY
David isn't hiding from me, I left him standing at the altar six years ago and now I'm...

ROSA
Fuck the details, they're *always* to blame... Look, too many of these guys duck out on us, especially after they become doctors or lawyers. I see it at my company all day long! So I'm just gonna make sure you get your, you know, fairy tale ending or whatever...
(BEAT)
One of us should.

BETTY
Rosa, I can't believe you're doing all this for me...thank you.

Rosa glances over to see Betty pass a business card to A WAITER who checks on them. When he is safely gone, Rosa touches Betty on the sleeve.

ROSA
Hey, how 'bout a card for me? What is that?
(takes one, reads)
"Please call if you have any information on David Ravell." This is *my* phone number! How many of these have you given out?

BETTY
How many men have I talked to?

ROSA
Jesus! They're all gonna be calling *me*!

BETTY
You said in L.A., anything goes.

ROSA
I was talking about what you could wear!

100 EXT. DESERT HIGHWAY - THE NEXT DAY 100

The Town Car's parked on a barren stretch of desert highway, white smoke billowing from the hood. Half a mile ahead Charlie and Wesley are walking in the sweltering heat.

They're in their shirtsleeves, drenched in sweat as the sun beats down on them.

CHARLIE
See, in a LeSabre Betty's probably getting twenty-two, maybe twenty-five miles to the gallon, where we're topping out at fifteen.
(BEAT)
She's probably all cool and fresh, and comfortable in that nice air-conditioned car right now.

Wesley wipes the sweat from his eyes and trudges on in silence. Charlie takes out a photo of Betty and speaks to it.

CHARLIE (cont'd)
You don't look comfortable *here*. That's 'cause you don't like being the center of attention, do you? Nah. You're like me.

WESLEY
What the hell's the matter with you?

Wesley grabs the photo, tears it in half and tosses it. Then he starts walking. Charlie is stunned for a moment, but recovers quickly. He finds the pieces and stuffs them in his pocket, then catches up to Wesley.

CHARLIE
That was a really shitty thing to do.

WESLEY
I'm sick of looking at her mother-fucking face.

A beat... they walk for a moment.

CHARLIE
Don't talk like that. She's my last one, Wesley, my final target.
(to photo)
Don't you realize your special, that you represent something?

This is too much. Wesley explodes.

WESLEY
What? What does she *represent*?! What could some cornbread white bitch from Kansas who's dragging our sorry asses up and down the Louisiana Purchase possibly mean to you?!! I'd just *love* to know...

CHARLIE
I dunno... something.
(BEAT)
Why is she doing this to me? Why?...

WESLEY
I don't know, but when we find her she's gonna die for it.

101-102 MOVED 101-102

102A INT. ROADSIDE GARAGE - LATE AFTERNOON 102A

The Lincoln Town Car is raised up high on the hydraulic jack. Wesley is at a pay phone out front.

WESLEY
Can you describe her to me?... Okay... Yeah, that sounds like her... Thanks.

He hangs up and goes into the garage, where he addresses the Town Car above him.

WESLEY (cont'd)
They found her in Vegas.

No answer.

WESLEY (cont'd)
Perfect match on the description.

ON CHARLIE

Lying across the front seat taping the reassembled photo of Betty to the dash. Charlie's beginning to come apart. His hair is uncombed and his clothes are wrinkled. His eyes have a thousand-yard stare.

WESLEY (O.S.)
Sounds like she's with the buyer Del lined up.

Charlie pulls himself up on the door and looks down.

CHARLIE
How'd they describe her?

WESLEY
You know, blonde, thin, whatever...

CHARLIE
Not so fast! Slower... 'blonde, thin', yes... Did they say she had style? A kind of grace or anything?

Wesley rolls his eyes, then goes straight to the levers controlling the hydraulic jack.

WESLEY
(to mechanic)
How do I get this fucking thing down?

MECHANIC
I wouldn't if I were you. He got pretty upset when I tried it...

103 INT. LAW OFFICE - A DIFFERENT DAY 103

MERCEDES LOPEZ, early 40's, impeccably dressed, enters her office loaded down with a bulging briefcase and a stack of files under her arms.

(*The entire scene is in Spanish*.)

MERCEDES
What do you think my father would do if I told him I didn't want to be a lawyer anymore?

ROSA
Probably the same thing my mom would do if I got engaged... have a heart attack.

MERCEDES
So how's it going with your new roomie? What's her name?

ROSA
Betty. It's O.K. except I'm worn out. We spent all weekend looking for her doctor-boy. How can a big time heart guy leave no trace of himself?

MERCEDES
So tell her to settle for the old one in
Orange County.

ROSA
She's gonna have to 'cause I'm out of
ideas.

MERCEDES
Maybe we're suing him for malpractice.
What's his name again?

ROSA
David Ravell.

MERCEDES
God, that sounds so familiar. Ravell,
Ravell... where's he out of?

ROSA
I'm not sure now. She said he used to be
over at Loma Vista. I never heard of it.

MERCEDES
Loma Vista?
(laughs)
You mean like the guy on "A Reason to
Love?"

104 INT. ROSA'S APARTMENT - LATER 104

Rosa enters, tosses her purse on the table and goes straight to the VCR. Written in magic marker on a video is "A Reason to Love, Apr. 23." The tape Sue Ann gave to Betty.

She pops it in and turns it on. The OPENING TITLES start ... The characters appear ... one is an impossibly handsome man over the title "DOCTOR DAVID RAVELL."

105 INT. HOSPITAL PHARMACY - LATER STILL 105

Betty working at a desk in the pharmacy. The same clerk as before busies himself at another counter. Rosa appears at the glass partition and raps urgently on it.

ROSA
Guess who I saw today.

BETTY
Who?

ROSA
Doctor David Ravell.

BETTY
What? Where was he?!

ROSA
ON TELEVISION!!
(off Betty's puzzled look)
Cut the shit, will you!

A BEAT. Rosa SLAMS the videotape down on the counter.

ROSA
Either you're making a fool out of me because you get off on it, or you got serious problems. Which one is it?!

BETTY
I have *no* idea what you're talking about.

ROSA
I'M TALKING ABOUT DAVID RAVELL!!

BETTY
Shhh! I heard you the first time.

ROSA
(suddenly calm)
I spent my weekend looking for someone who does - not - exist. I should have been here at the hospital with my brother, but I was with you.

BETTY
If you didn't want to do it, you should have said so! Is this about gas money?

ROSA
IT'S NOT ABOUT GAS MONEY!!
(BEAT)
You have a thing for an actor on a stupid white soap opera, and we searched all over town for his character! Not the *actor* - whose name is George, by the way. His *character!*

Rosa stands over Betty, fuming.

BETTY
Are you having a nervous breakdown?

Rosa SCREAMS and smacks her hand on the glass as Betty watches. SEVERAL PEOPLE in a nearby lounge look up. Rosa stares at them until they look away.

BETTY (cont'd)
Why'd you help me in the first place?

ROSA
I helped you because I'm an idiot! Ask my mother, I *love* it when people take advantage of me! I TRUSTED YOU!! I THOUGHT HE WAS REAL!

BETTY
HE *IS* REAL!!

Betty tries to return to her work but Rosa confronts her loudly. The nearby VISITORS and STAFF pretend to be busy.

ROSA
You need help, Betty! Even if this is your idea of a joke, you need SERIOUS HELP!!
(walking away - to herself)
Necesitas un médico! Prontísimo!

ON BETTY

fuming in her humiliation. After a moment, Rosa reappears at the window.

ROSA (cont'd)
I'm not going back on our arrangement. My word is good, and my family owes you. But I think it's best for both of us if you get your own place as soon as you can.

BETTY
Fine.

106 OMIT (NOW 102A) 106

106A EXT. SIZEMORE MOTORS - KANSAS - NIGHT 106A

Roy and Joyce approach the door to the trailer/office. She takes out her key, then stops. It's been padlocked and barred with yellow police tape, as is the whole lot. Roy pulls hard on the lock, then starts looking around.

JOYCE
You're wastin' your time, Roy.

ROY
Look Joyce, I need your key to the files, not advice, okay? This is a complex case.

Roy works on opening a side window.

JOYCE
Nothin' complex about it. Del's dead, Betty's gone. She's probably dead, too.

ROY
You'd like that wouldn't you? You've hated Betty since you were in Pep Squad together...

JOYCE
No... before that.

ROY
Ahh, I hate this town! Places like this just make you small...
(BEAT)
I should have never come back here after college.

JOYCE
Blah - blah - blah... Hurry up, will ya, I got a date tonight...

Roy forces the glass open and starts to squirm through the window as Joyce watches.

JOYCE (cont'd)
I don't know what you think you'll find, anyway.

ROY (O.S.)
Names, a phone number, something...
(BEAT)
Listen, Ballard told me that the guy who brought the missing car down from Detroit was murdered, but do you see him doing anything about it? If Ballard wasn't such a stubborn ass, I wouldn't have to be breaking in here...

The color drains from Joyce's face.

JOYCE
What did you say?

ROY (O.S.)
The driver was killed. I think there's a connection--

JOYCE
(starting to cry)
No, about... Are you talking about Duane Cooley?

ROY (O.S.)
Yeah. Why, you know him?

JOYCE
(crying)
Know him? We were gonna get married! He was gonna leave his wife for me! Fuck!!...

Joyce begins to sob at the side of the trailer as Roy shimmies through the window frame.

Suddenly, Ballard is there, weapon cocked and placed roughly into Roy's privates. Joyce backs away.

BALLARD
I know you don't use them, but if you wanna keep 'em you'll back out of there slowly...

106B INT. SQUADCAR - MOVING - NIGHT 106B

Roy is in the rear of the car, handcuffed to the screen dividing the front seat from the back. Ballard is driving.

ROY
Come on, Elden, think about it. The driver, all them trunks standing open like that... something's going on here!

BALLARD
I know that...

ROY
Well, do something, then, damnit!

BALLARD
You watch your mouth when you're in a goddamn county vehicle... You don't think I see what's going on? Del, now this Cooley fella, both of 'em mixed up with Joyce... 'S not no conspiracy, not some episode off the X-Files... 's just a crime of passion, plain and simple. Betty's on some kind'a pre-minstral rampage, *that's* what is going on here.

A moment of silence as they drive.

ROY
Oww... Did you have to make these things so tight?

BALLARD
No, I didn't *have* to.

He grins at Roy in the rearview mirror.

107 INT. LAW FIRM - ANOTHER DAY 107

Mercedes Lopez arrives at the office and stops at Rosa's desk.

(The entire scene is in Spanish)

MERCEDES
Hey... Is Betty still trying to find that soap opera guy?

ROSA
Oh, yeah... Man, I'd love to find that actor just to see the look on her face, watch her bubble burst in mid-air.

Mercedes hands her two tickets to a benefit.

MERCEDES
Here's your needle... He's supposed to make an appearance here tonight.

108 INT. BETTY'S BEDROOM - LATER 108

Betty's lying on her bed reading "Modern Nurse". The L.A. Times Classifieds are open on the bed. Rosa looks in.

BETTY
Don't worry, I'm looking... just taking a tiny break.

ROSA
This is crazy. I come home, you go to your room. You go in the kitchen, I go to my room. It's stupid.

Betty nods in agreement.

ROSA (cont'd)
So what do you say? Can we be friends?

BETTY
...okay.

Rosa smiles and starts looking at the tickets in her hand.

BETTY (cont'd)
What are those for?

ROSA
Oh, it's a charity dinner. The money goes to a good cause, but I don't have anybody to go with...

BETTY
Umm...

Rosa exits for a moment, then reappears in the doorway.

ROSA
...you hungry at all?

109 INT. LINCOLN TOWN CAR - MOVING - LATE AFTERNOON 109

The car is covered in dust and mud from the road. It's worse inside: food wrappers, empty bottles, pieces of clothing, filthy windows. They've been living in it.

Wesley's driving now. Charlie's almost unrecognizable: a six-day beard, uncombed greasy hair, bloodshot eyes, rumpled clothes and an exhausted, faraway look. The photo of Betty faces him, taped to the glove box. He is reading from the diary, which he clutches like the Bible.

They roar along a desert highway, passing a sign that says "Grand Canyon, This Exit. 74 Miles." Charlie looks up, marking his place.

CHARLIE
We should go.

WESLEY
We don't have time to look at a hole in the ground. We can make Vegas in four hours. This one's got to be her.

CHARLIE
It's a very moving experience, trust me.

WESLEY
No.

CHARLIE
One of the Seven Natural Wonders of the World.

WESLEY
No... be dark before we get there. You wanna see the Grand Canyon at *night*?

CHARLIE
What difference does it make? She wasn't in Kansas City, or Houston, or Dallas. We
(MORE)

CHARLIE (cont'd)
went to every goddamn place Del mentioned and no Betty. So what the hell makes you think she's in Vegas? You think she's waiting for us with tassles on her titties? Vegas is too crass for Betty.

WESLEY
I said, 'No.' N-O.

Charlie turns to a passage and reads aloud.

CHARLIE
"When I grow up I'm going to become a nurse or a veterinarian. I always want to help people and value all life, be it animal, plant or mineral..."
(to Wesley)
Does that sound like a goddamn *showgirl* to you?

WESLEY
Do you hear yourself right now...? Like a fucking *madman*...

Wesley drives on stoically. The Exit comes and goes.

CHARLIE
Every American should see the Grand Canyon. Are you an American?

WESLEY
Yes, I am and we're not going. Act professional.

Charlie stares at him, hate rising from just below the surface. He draws a nickel-plated pistol and points it at Wesley's head. Wesley looks at it and keeps on driving.

Charlie knows this isn't the way to handle it. He lowers the pistol.

CHARLIE
If you don't take the next turn for the canyon, I'm blowing my goddamn brains all over this car.

He puts the pistol in his mouth and cocks it. Wesley looks over, not so sure this time.

LONG SHOT of the black Town Car as the turn signal comes on, and it eases onto a lonely dirt road. Their headlights pick out a sign that says: "Grand Canyon Fire Trail. Forestry Personnel Only."

110 EXT. BEVERLY HILTON - EVENING 110

Rosa and Betty approach the hotel entrance. Ahead of them a black Lincoln Town Car pulls up. Headlights glint on the chrome, hitting Betty in the eye. She freezes, and Rosa bumps into her.

ROSA
Sorry.

Betty stares at the car, unable to remember what it should mean. Then a MAN in a tuxedo gets out. Betty moves on.

111 INT. BEVERLY HILTON - LOBBY - EVENING 111

A sign on an easel reads "Save the Children." Betty and Rosa present their tickets at the door to a ballroom.

Several times there is a stir near the entrance and a scattering of flashbulbs. Rosa scans the crowd.

BETTY
Looking for someone?

ROSA
You never know who you'll see.

Rosa keeps looking. Finally, GEORGE McCORD - the actor who plays DAVID RAVELL - enters.

He comes in with LYLA BRANCH, late 40's, and TWO OTHER MEN. Several women approach George, some starry-eyed, for quick, polite greetings. He's doing his job of being a soap star.

Rosa waits for an opening, then puts her hands on Betty's shoulders and points her at George.

ROSA (cont'd)
Look who's here!

Betty's jaw drops. She freezes.

ROSA (cont'd)
What are you waiting for? Talk to him!
You came fifteen hundred miles for this.

Rosa prods her, then Betty makes her way unsteadily toward George. When she's a few feet away he looks up.

He can't help but notice her - she's beautiful. She's also looking right into his eyes. The conversation stops as he does a double take in Betty's direction.

GEORGE
Do I know you from...?

His friends watch as George studies her face.

BETTY
...of course you do.
(hurt)
You don't remember me?

GEORGE
I take it I should. I'm sorry.

BETTY
We were engaged.

LYLA
Oh good, another one...

George's friends look at each other. A few heads turn.

GEORGE
I beg your pardon?

BETTY
But I'm the one who's sorry. Letting you go was the biggest mistake of my life.
(to his friends)
We were thirteen days away from getting married and ... I just got scared. It's a mistake I've had to live with for six years. But it's behind me now...
(to George)
And I hope you can put it behind you. I've missed you... David.

George sighs with relief. His friends smile. The tension evaporates. They can handle a fanatical fan.

GEORGE
That's very kind of you.

BETTY
The day I left you I just drove and drove. I drove all day and all that night, and I didn't go anywhere. I just kept driving. I stopped at a little country church, and the pastor let me in, and I sat--

LYLA
... in the very first pew, where we would have sat on our wedding day.

Betty looks at her. So does George.

LYLA (cont'd)
I can't believe I remembered that, although I suppose I should. I wrote it...
(to Betty)
But that was seven years ago, and you're quoting it verbatim. I'm flattered... I think. Or frightened. What's your name?

BETTY
Betty Sizemore. What do you mean you wrote it?

LYLA
I'm Lyla Branch. I'm the Producer.

They shake hands. ACROSS THE ROOM Rosa watches expectantly.

LYLA (cont'd)
Alright, I admit it, you had me there. You're better than most of them, anyway...do you have a headshot?

GEORGE
No, wait...what happened next, Betty?

LYLA
Are you sure you want to encourage this?
(BEAT)
No, you're right, let's have some fun. So, what did happened next, "Betty"?

BETTY
Well, David moved out here and started his residency. Then he met Leslie--

LYLA
No, no, no. We know all that. What happened with you?

BETTY
I married a car salesman.

The friends laugh. Rosa watches, confused. So is Betty.

FRIEND #1
You were dumped for a car salesman, George!

BETTY
Why are you calling him George?

FRIEND #2
Yeah - David - tell us about this car salesman.

George likes the challenge. This party isn't so boring after all.

GEORGE
Oh, you mean Fred.

BETTY
No, Del.

GEORGE
Right, Del. Del was one hot salesman. Of cars. He could talk anyone into anything.

BETTY
You knew Del?!

GEORGE
Honey, I didn't want to tell you at the time, but Del and I go way back. We went to school together. In fact, he saved my life. Two more minutes in that icy water and I would have drowned. But Del jumped in and grabbed me. We fell out of touch eventually, but I still owe him one.

BETTY
He never told me anything about...that's unbelievable!

LYLA
Funny, that's just what I was thinking...

GEORGE
I can't tell you how much it hurts me to hear that you married him.

His friends snicker. Rosa stares. Betty is oblivious to everything but George.

BETTY
I'm *so* sorry. Life makes us do awful things sometimes.

She's ready to cry. Which only inspires him all the more.

GEORGE
I tried to tell myself it was for the best, that there was a reason behind it. But... Del?

BETTY
There was no plan! I was just young and stupid and scared!

GEORGE
You never gave us a chance...

BETTY
I know that. I can't tell you how many times I've said that to myself in those exact words.

Betty wipes her tears away as they flow freely now. George doesn't like seeing her cry; he tries to say something but his friends interrupt.

GEORGE
Hey, don't... come on, I was just... you're not really crying, are you?... I was just playing along...

FRIEND #1
Now, look what you've done, George.

BETTY
Why do they keep calling you George?

GEORGE
I don't know. Why do you keep calling me George?

LYLA
Listen - David - It's getting late.

George hesitates; Lyla sees it.

GEORGE
(to Betty)
Right, uhh...I feel terrible about this, we have a prior engagement at another party.
(BEAT)
But... I'd be honored if you'd come.

LYLA
Yeah, bring your friend along. I'm sure you got a lot of catching up to do...

Rosa watches, stunned, as Betty waves to her as she leaves arm-in-arm with the man of her dreams.

112 EXT. GRAND CANYON - NIGHT 112

The Town Car is parked near one of the viewing stops at the rim. Charlie stands in the darkness, but Wesley stays in the car.

CHARLIE
You don't know what you're missing, asshole.

Charlie walks toward the canyon rim. Suddenly, Betty appears in the headlights standing at the rail - her back to Charlie - with a bouquet of flowers.

ON WESLEY

Just as he closes his eyes to rest, the CAR PHONE RINGS.

WESLEY
Yeah?

SUE ANN (V.O.)
Mr. Campbell?

WESLEY
Huh?

SUE ANN (V.O.)
Is this Neighborly Life Insurance?

WESLEY
(recovering)
Oh, umm, yes, this is Dwight Campbell.

SUE ANN (V.O.)
It's Sue Ann Rogers, Betty Sizemore's friend? I heard from her.

ON CHARLIE

walking toward the rail. As he nears her, they kiss.

Suddenly, REPEATED BLASTS from the car horn.

The image of Betty shudders, then blurs, then fades away entirely. Charlie rubs at his eyes tiredly, then slowly trudges back toward the car.

Charlie returns and gets into the car. Silence. Wesley stares at him.

WESLEY
... you have a good time? You make a little wish?

Silence from Charlie.

WESLEY (cont'd)
Well, guess what? I found Betty... where she's been, anyway.

CHARLIE
Where? Where is she?

WESLEY
I'm not telling.

CHARLIE
What?

WESLEY
I'm not telling 'til you straighten up. You been acting like fucking Jerry Lewis on me and this shit's gotta stop or you can forget about your Betty... I mean it.

A slow transformation comes over Charlie.

CHARLIE
Wesley, I'm fine... just tell me where she is.

113 EXT. BEVERLY HILTON - NIGHT 113

George, Betty, Lyla and the two friends are waiting outside the hotel for their cars.

FRIEND #2
I bought a car from Del, too. He sold me a lemon.

LYLA
Really? I put a hundred and thirty thousand miles on mine.

BETTY
Huh. I had no idea our little lot was so popular...

FRIEND #1
I never bought a car from Del. But I loved him. In my own way.

GEORGE
I guess we all did. (to Betty) You know, I didn't marry Leslie because I loved her. I married her to forget you...

BETTY
Oh, David...I'm sorry I caused you that much pain.

A black jeep 4x4 pulls up and ERIC AUGUSTINO, the actor who plays LONNIE, gets out.

BETTY (cont'd)
Oh my God! What's Lonnie doing here?

GEORGE
You're late, Eric.

ERIC
I know. Why are you guys leaving?

LYLA
We did our twenty minutes.

Before Eric can take another step Betty SLAPS him across the face. FLASHBULBS go off as PHOTOGRAPHERS capture the moment.

BETTY
You bastard! How can you even show your face around here? Do you think we're not onto you?

ERIC
Who the hell is this?

GEORGE
Sorry. She thinks you're someone else.

George hustles Betty to his car as photographers continue to shoot.

BETTY
I know exactly who you are!

114 EXT. CANYON RANCH BAR - NIGHT 114

The Lincoln Town Car rumbles into the dusty parking lot and parks.

CHARLIE
This doesn't look like the kind of place Betty would go to.

WESLEY
Maybe she had to use the bathroom. She pees, doesn't she?!...

Wesley tears the photo of Betty from the glove box.

CHARLIE
Be careful with that!

Charlie takes it back and gingerly secures the tape.

115 INT. CANYON RANCH BAR - NIGHT 115

Merle is at the bar, drunk, the only customer on a slow night. Ellen drops two coasters in front of Charlie and Wesley as they sit down.

ELLEN
What can I get you?

WESLEY
We're Federal Marshals, ma'am.

Ellen looks dubiously at their unshaven faces and rumpled clothes.

CHARLIE
We're looking for this young lady.

He slides the photo of Betty across the bar. Ellen's gaze drops to the picture for a second, and Charlie sees what he was looking for - a flicker of recognition. He allows himself a satisfied grin.

Wesley shows Ellen his badge as Merle checks out the photo.

ELLEN
I haven't seen her.

MERLE
Sure you have! That's ...

ELLEN
Shut up, Merle.

Charlie continues to grin at Ellen ...

WESLEY
Ma'am, if you've seen this woman--

MERLE
Betty! That's her name - Betty.

Charlie takes the photo and puts it back in his pocket.

ELLEN
I never saw that woman before, and neither has Merle. He drinks too much. And don't try to tell me you're cops. I
(MORE)

ELLEN (cont'd)
was married to a cop for nine years, and you're not cops. Now get out of here.

Wesley steps behind Merle, takes a handful of his hair and SLAMS his head into the popcorn machine on the bar. Merle staggers away, stunned. Wesley removes the tin popcorn scoop from a nearby hook.

Ellen reaches for something under the bar, but Charlie's faster. He pins her arm with one hand.

CHARLIE
You haven't been very forthcoming with us.

They watch Wesley follow Merle at a slow walk around the pool table, CLOBBERING him over the head about every five steps with the popcorn scoop.

Merle wobbles with every shot, but won't go down. They begin a torturous second lap around the table, punctuated by the CLANG of the scoop against Merle's head.

CHARLIE
What's your name, dear?

ELLEN
Ellen.

CHARLIE
That's a nice name.

After one more CLANGING shot Merle staggers, then falls. Wesley walks over to Charlie and Ellen, drawing his knife.

WESLEY
That's a really nice name...

116 INT. GEORGE'S RANGE ROVER - MOVING - LATER - NIGHT 116

George and Betty are alone.

BETTY
Lyla's very nice.

GEORGE
Yes, she is.

BETTY
She told me I was charming and relentless, and would go far in this town. And she said that unlike the other charming, relentless people she knew, she liked me.

GEORGE
She's a good person to know.
(BEAT)
So where did you study again?

BETTY
Carleton School of Nursing. Two semesters, but Del made me give it up...

GEORGE
Alright, okay... I think you broke the record for staying in character about three hours ago.

BETTY
You told me that two hours ago.

He pulls up in front of Rosa's apartment and parks.

BETTY (cont'd)
I haven't been this happy since I was twelve years old.

GEORGE
What happened when you were twelve?

BETTY
For Mother's Day, I used all my allowance that I'd been saving to take my mother to Kansas City. We got our nails done and had lunch at "Skies," a restaurant at the top of a building from where you can see the whole city. It was the last outing we took together. She died the following year.

GEORGE
Wow ... You just gave me goosebumps, you know that? You make it all sound so real. Great improv...

BETTY
I just want everything to be perfect between us.

GEORGE
I know. Listen, we need to take a time-out here. Can we talk seriously for a minute?

BETTY
Of course.

GEORGE
At last! I know how much you want this. You're gifted and *extremely* determined, but ... it's not up to me.

BETTY
I know. It's up to us.

Betty leans over and kisses George - so deeply that he's too surprised to react. She pulls away abruptly and gets out.

BETTY (cont'd)
I love you, David. And I want to see you tomorrow, and the next day, and the next day.

Still surprised, and now a little intrigued, he watches her go inside.

117 INT. ROSA'S KITCHEN - NIGHT 117

Betty comes in and pours a drink from the fridge. Rosa appears in a nightshirt behind her, framed in the doorway.

ROSA
Were you with him this whole time?

BETTY
Oh, God! You scared me! Yes...

ROSA
You still in love?

Betty nods.

ROSA
Does he know you think he's real?

BETTY
He *is* real.

ROSA
Uh-huh... So, what'd you talk about?

BETTY
Oh, my gosh, everything! My trip out here, what we've both been doing, you know...

ROSA
No, I'm not sure I could begin to imagine... So, where'd you go?

BETTY
To a party in the Hollywood Hills.

ROSA
Was it a huge place? With a view of the whole world?

BETTY
Yes. I'd never been in a place like that before.

ROSA
I have, lots of times. My mother used to clean them. I used to piss in their pools.

Rosa gets up and starts for her bedroom. She stops.

ROSA (cont'd)
This isn't fair, you know. Do you always get what you want?

BETTY
No, almost never.

ROSA
But, you're in love with someone who doesn't exist. You come here, you meet this guy, who *should* laugh in your face, and instead you leave with him!
(BEAT)
Betty, you are one-of-a-kind...

Rosa goes into her bedroom and closes the door. Betty smiles and nods, sipping at her drink as she retires to her room.

118 OMIT (NOW 120A) 118

119 INT. POLICE STATION - JAIL CELL - THE NEXT DAY 119

From his cell Roy Ostrey hears a door open, then the sound of approaching footsteps. It's Ballard.

ROY
Elden, let me out of here. Now! This is ridiculous, I need medical attention!

BALLARD
That's a nice name for what you need...

ROY
Come on, I have to get this dressing off...it itches! And what about my fish? Who is taking care of them?

Ballard doesn't say anything. He's very grim, subdued. Roy has never seen him like this.

BALLARD
Just shut up a second and listen... That, uh... that bar in Arizona? Where you said Betty was?

ROY
What about it?

BALLARD
Any idea where it is?

ROY
Little place called "Williams," why?

BALLARD
I just got something off the wire. The woman who owns it was murdered last night.
(BEAT)
Now, I'm not saying I agree with you or nothing, but... what else do you know?

ROY
I know plenty.

120 EXT. LYLA'S HOUSE - DAY 120

Palatial, spartan. Lyla is sitting in the inner court of her Lloyd Wright home with George at one knee.

GEORGE
She makes me stretch! I got inside my character last night like I haven't done in six years on "Reason". It was a totally rejuvenating experience.

LYLA
I know, George, I was there. I'm not denying that she's good.

GEORGE
She's even taken a *job* as a nurse!
(BEAT)
David Ravell's getting boring, Lyla.

LYLA
We know that...

GEORGE
Can I have an evil twin?

LYLA
No, George, we've already done that with Lonnie. The blind one last year, remember?

GEORGE
Oh, of course. Who can forget the Emmy?
(BEAT)
Then let me bring Betty to the set and see what happens.

LYLA
I don't know, George...

GEORGE
I'll tell the cast ahead of time. What do you say?

LYLA
I'll think about it.

GEORGE
It'll be like live television! Let's live on the edge a little. You and I can break the mold here!

LYLA
I said I'll think about it.

GEORGE
Fine, but promise me one thing. If we use her, I want to direct those episodes. She's my discovery.

LYLA
Actually, she was my discovery... just like you.

GEORGE
Hmm?

LYLA
"Would you like ground pepper on that salad, Ms. Branch?" Remember?

GEORGE
... yeah.

120A EXT. L.A. FREEWAY - NIGHT 120A

The black Lincoln Town car hurdles along the 10 Freeway, a revitalized Charlie back at the wheel. Surrounded by traffic, the lights of the city in the distance, the two men push on toward their new destination.

121 EXT. HOLLYWOOD MOTEL - THE NEXT DAY 121

The black Lincoln Town Car - now washed and gleaming - is parked in front of a modest motel.

122 INT. HOLLYWOOD MOTEL / BATHROOM - DAY 122

Charlie looks like a new man - showered, clear-eyed and energized - he's at the sink shaving as Wesley watches from his seat on the edge of the bathtub.

CHARLIE
So you believed the bartender. Why?

WESLEY
Well... I think I saw her soul.

CHARLIE
That's good. You're learning. But let me tell you why I know she was lying.
(BEAT)
First off, Betty would never fall for a soap star. It's beneath her.

WESLEY
I dunno, that lady sounded pretty sure...

CHARLIE
No, no, Betty came here strictly for business, 'cause it's the biggest market for what she's selling. I should have known it all along. I'm kicking myself as I shave here. So, first thing we...

WESLEY
Wait, wait, wait a minute... that doesn't make sense.

CHARLIE
What doesn't?

WESLEY
You gimme this bullshit Psychic Friends theory, you believe that dumbshit trucker, you believe this woman...

CHARLIE
I never said that I believed...

WESLEY
No, you believed her, we drove all the way to L.A. so that means you trusted her that much... so why's the rest of her story suddenly so kooky? Huh?

CHARLIE
'Cause I just don't buy it. Call it instinct. Call it 35 years of professional know-how...

WESLEY
I call it 'nutty' as my shit after I eat Almond Roca...

CHARLIE
You need to remember who you're talking to...

WESLEY
I need to get my goddamn head examined.
(BEAT)
You can't rule something out on a whim. Or because she's cute. I've been following your whims all across the U.S. of A. and now *I'm* tired! Me!

CHARLIE
Wesley...

WESLEY
"It's beneath her..." She's a mother-fucking *housewife*... nothing's beneath her!

Wesley stands up for emphasis, pointing a finger in Charlie's personal space. Charlie reacts at this, throwing his razor into the sink and turning on Wesley.

CHARLIE
Boy, you need to get outta my face... now! You got a feeling, then you do what you gotta do, but don't you *ever* try to tell me my job. Not ever.

It's a standoff. Wesley blinks first. He stalks off and out of sight. In a moment, he returns.

WESLEY
Fine. Just fine... I'll go check some shit on my own then. And don't call me 'boy...'

He turns and slams into the door frame. He glares at Charlie, then exits. When the front door BANGS SHUT allows himself to go back to his shaving.

123 EXT. STUDIO BUILDINGS - DAY 123

Map in hand, Wesley stand near A GUARD and discreetly asks questions.

WESLEY
... what kinda car's Jasmine drive?

GUARD
Ahh, Mercedes, I think. Black.

WESLEY
Yeah? The sport utility?

GUARD
Uh-huh.

WESLEY
Damn, that's sweet...
(BEAT)
She really that good-looking in person?

GUARD
Better.

WESLEY
Oh fuck...

Wesley looks around covertly, then produces a fifty.

WESLEY (cont'd)
Hey, can you sneak me on the lot?

GUARD
Sure.

Wesley smiles and wanders off, headed toward a series of studio buildings in the distance. The guard watches him go.

GUARD (cont'd)
... it's Sunday, I can sneak anybody on the lot.

124 INT. HOLLYWOOD MOTEL ROOM - DAY 124

Charlie toys with matches from the Canyon Ranch Bar. Working off a list of names and phone numbers from his Zaurus, he makes calls from his room.

CHARLIE
Betty Sizemore, she's got ten kilos... Blonde hair, a great figure... sort of a whole Doris Day thing going on. That's what I said-- *Doris Day*. You could see her working at the U.N., or something. 'The U.N.' "United Nations." Forget it...
(BEAT)
Nobody like that? You're sure? Yeah, Detroit by way of Kansas... Alright, let me know if you hear anything, okay?

He hangs up. Deletes another one off the list and looks out the window. Checks the now well-worn photo of Betty. He's starting to doubt himself.

125 INT. ROSA'S APARTMENT / BATHROOM - EVENING 125

Rosa stands in the doorway as Betty, wearing one of Rosa's hotter outfits, puts on her makeup.

BETTY
Are you sure I can borrow this?

ROSA
No, please. Go ahead, it's your funeral...

BETTY
Rosa...

ROSA
Well, what if this guy's just playing with you? What if he's lying about who he is?

BETTY
You should have a little faith in people.

ROSA
Does he ever talk about medicine? His patients, the hospital?

BETTY
All the time. It's always "Loma Vista" this, "Loma Vista" that.

The DOORBELL RINGS. Rosa goes to the front door and looks through the peephole, then opens the door. George McCord, flowers in hand, gives his best leading man smile.

GEORGE
You must be Rosa. I've heard so much about you... I'm George McCord.

ROSA
Not as much as I've heard about you. She's a very nice girl and you better not hurt her.

GEORGE
What?

Betty appears.

BETTY
Rosa, so you've met David?

ROSA
Sure did! And a funny thing, Betty, he introduced himself to me as *George*!

BETTY
Oh, he does that.
(hugging him)
It's this silly game he plays. Half the people who know him call him George.

126 EXT. ROSA'S APARTMENT - NIGHT 126

GEORGE
I don't think your friend likes me.

BETTY
She's a little jealous, I think. And confused when it comes to men...
(BEAT)
So where are we going?

GEORGE
Well, first I thought Patina, and then the Ivy, but then I thought of somewhere a little more romantic. Like my place.

127 INT. GEORGE'S HOUSE - NIGHT 127

Modern glass and steel structure in the hills. Austere. Betty and George sit on the sofa with the lights low and SOFT MUSIC playing.

GEORGE
God, I haven't felt like this since I was with Stella Adler in New York. You're so...real.

He leans forward slowly to kiss her, but Betty pulls back.

BETTY
You never mentioned a 'Stella' to me.

GEORGE
Didn't I?

BETTY
No, I would have remembered that name.
The only Stella I ever knew was a parrot.
(BEAT)
Was this before Leslie? Before us?...

George takes her face in his hands and looks at her.

GEORGE
I've never met anyone like you, Betty.

BETTY
I know, that's why we were meant to be together...

GEORGE
No, I mean your dedication scares me...

BETTY
It's easy to be dedicated, when you care about something...

GEORGE
Yeah, I felt that way, too, when I first started, but now... the hours, the repetition... it's not all glamour and mall openings anymore. Maybe I should've listened to my people and tried to make the crossover to nights earlier, I don't know...
(BEAT)
...I just hope it's not too late for me. God! Listen to me, "Me, me, me." It's so easy to get caught up in the whole ego cycle of this business and make it all about yourself. Stop, right? That's it, no more about me tonight, I promise... Let's talk about you...what do you think about me? I'm kidding... Seriously, Betty, I'm doing all the talking here...

BETTY
...but I love listening to you, so that's okay...

GEORGE
Thanks. But I'd like to hear what you're feeling...

BETTY
Well, I just feel that life'll be much sweeter for you now with me around. I promise...

GEORGE
You know, I almost believe that... you're like a warm breeze that's suddenly blown into my life...
(laughs)
I said that to Leslie, once, at her funeral, remember?...

BETTY
I remember. You said it to her, but it was meant for me, wasn't it?

GEORGE
Yes... maybe it was.

She kisses him deeply, then allows herself to fall back on the sofa, pulling George down on top of her and kissing him passionately.

128 INT. HOLLYWOOD MOTEL - THE NEXT DAY 128

Wesley hands Charlie a newspaper folded open to the Entertainment section, where there is a picture of Betty slapping the actor Eric Augustino. George is in b.g.

WESLEY
...so I'm standing there, minding my own business on Hollywood Blvd., checking out Gladys Knight's star-thing there, I look up at this little souvenir shop dude, Chinese dude, reading a paper... and who do I see?
(holding up paper)
That's Lonnie. He's the show's Main Prick. And that is *definitely* Betty. Now, that ain't no coincidence...
(BEAT)
I found out where they shoot it, and where the dressing rooms are.

Charlie studies the photo, troubled by something.

CHARLIE
Who's this?

WESLEY
A doctor on the show... why?

Charlie thinks about it, then reaches into his pocket and takes out the photo of Betty with the cardboard David. As he compares the photos, Wesley peeks over his shoulder.

WESLEY (cont'd)
What in the...
(simmering)
What the *hell* is this? You've been holding out on me. All this fucking time!

CHARLIE
It just didn't fit her profile...

WESLEY
Fuck the profile! That's the same guy!!

CHARLIE
She can't be here because of a... a soap opera. Not a *soap opera*. That'd make her...

WESLEY
... crazy! No shit, Shaft!! And you ain't far behind...

CHARLIE
... but she's, no, Betty's smarter than that. She wouldn't be here for a...

WESLEY
I do not know how the fuck you lasted an hour in this job! Dragging our asses around with the *answer* to our prayers in your motherfucking jacket... a picture of that cunt right next to the...

Charlie cuts Wesley short by grabbing his shirt and pulling him close.

CHARLIE
Don't Don't you talk about Betty like that. I don't care who she ends up being, you never use that word again. Got it?

WESLEY
Man, you have got to get some therapy.

CHARLIE
I said 'got it?'

WESLEY
... yeah, I got it.
(struggling)
Come on, you're stretching out my vest...

CHARLIE
You made your point...
(drops him)
I was wrong.

He carefully folds the paper, pockets the photo and straightens his clothing. He straps on his holster and checks his weapon for emphasis.

CHARLIE (cont'd)
Now, get yourself ready.

129 INT. MOTEL BATHROOM - DAY 129

Wesley gathering his gear through the open door. Charlie stands looking at himself in the mirror. Touches at the gray in his hair. As an afterthought, he tosses on a splash of cologne.

130 OMIT 130

131 INT. SOUNDSTAGE - DAY 131

George leads Betty past several standing sets and into the 'operating room' as CREW MEMBERS buzz around. Betty walks with her eyes closed and holding George's hand.

GEORGE
Just a little further... come on...

George stops and puts both hands over Betty's eyes. He looks about expectantly and then uncovers them with a flourish.

GEORGE (cont'd)
Surprise!

Betty stares, slowly trying to take in her new surroundings. It looks like Loma Vista, but something is different. Odd. Cameras, lights, etc. - all the apparatus of a TV show - are in plain sight... And very disorienting.

BETTY
Oh my gosh...I didn't know I was going to meet your friends today...I dressed a little casual.

He leads her to a taped mark on the floor as CAST MEMBERS appear, including JASMINE and BLAKE DANIELS.

GEORGE
That's cute...listen, you got the part, and *I'm* *directing*. You've only got four lines today, so I thought I'd just spring it on you. No blocking or anything, just stand near the nurse's station... we're gonna do a quick walk-through. Alright?

He kisses her cheek and walks off toward the waiting Lyla before she can respond.

VOICE (O.S.)
Quiet on the set!

GEORGE
Traffic was terrible...

LYLA
No, that's fine, we've only got seventy pages to shoot...take your time.

A STAGE MANAGER hands Betty a set of sides and an on-set COSTUMER tries to fit her.

BETTY
Excuse me. What are you doing?

STAGE MANAGER
We'll get you into hair and make-up after this, just put this on...

The other actors take their positions. Lyla watches from behind the cameras as David readies himself. Chloe enters the set with Kleenex tucked into the neck of her costume.

CHLOE
(to Betty)
Hi. I hear you're great. Good luck...

BETTY
What are *you* doing here? David...

GEORGE
Your lines'll are in the script, but you can ad lib.

BETTY
Ad lib?

GEORGE
In fact, I *want* you to ad lib, that's the magic I'm after. I wanna give a whole new feel to the show.

She's sliding toward a complete meltdown.

VOICE
Slate it!

George steps back behind the cameras. Betty's still frozen to her spot, overwhelmed.

GEORGE
Just do what you've been doing. Watch the scene and on your cue take off from there.

VOICE
5-4-3-2...

Chloe and Blake run through their lines lifelessly, then stop when they get to Betty's cue. Their faces loom around her menacingly. Staring. The lights are impossibly bright. People begin to shuffle and stare at one another. Lyla clears her throat as George bounds on stage, still smiling.

GEORGE
Betty?

CHLOE
Are you all right?

BLAKE
(to Chloe)
I think you stepped on my first line...

CHLOE
... I was talking to her.
(to Betty)
Do you need anything...?

She's freezing up. George approaches her.

GEORGE
Betty, I thought this would be the best way. You know, throw you into it...

LYLA
What the hell's going on?

GEORGE
If you need a minute, that's okay. But I thought you'd want to--

BETTY
David, I don't... Can we talk privately for a second?

GEORGE
Stop calling me David. We're on set, for Christ's sake, you don't have to call me David here.

As he pulls away Betty grabs his arm.

BETTY
Why are you doing this to me?

GEORGE
Why am I doing this to you? Isn't this what you wanted?

Lyla approaches.

LYLA
Is there a problem, George?

GEORGE
No! No problem, there is no...
(to Betty, sotto)
What is the *problem*? Just do that... *thing*... you do! Come on! You drove me nuts with this for three days, now do it!

George steps back behind the cameras as if nothing's wrong. Betty still hasn't moved. She's shaking with fear. The cast and crew members find it hard to look at her.

LYLA
All right, everybody! That's ten minutes!

GEORGE
No! Let me try this!

JASMINE
(storming off)
This is bullshit!

LYLA
Forget it, George. It was a gamble, it didn't work. Nice try.

GEORGE
Let me try this, goddamnit! SHE'S BEEN DOING IT ALL WEEK, SHE CAN DO IT NOW!

LYLA
I SAID FORGET IT!

George throws down his script and rushes up to Betty, who reaches out to him. He brushes her hands away.

GEORGE
Well, I don't know what you had in mind, but I hope you're happy. I put myself on the line for you, my reputation, and you're making me look like an idiot.

BETTY
What do you mean? What did I do to you...

GEORGE
Who put you up to this? Did my ex-wife ask you to...?

BETTY
David, please--

GEORGE
STOP CALLING ME THAT! MY NAME IS NOT DAVID, AND IF YOU REALLY DON'T KNOW THE DIFFERENCE, YOU'RE MORE FUCKED UP THAN I THOUGHT YOU WERE!

Betty begins to cry.

STAGEHAND
Leave her alone, George!

GEORGE
SHUT THE FUCK UP!! You're a fucking grip, go *grip* something!!!
(to Betty)
And you're not an actress, you're nothing but a soap opera groupie, aren't you? YOU HAVE NOTHING BETTER TO DO! DO YOU?? Well, why don't you get a fucking life, and stop ruining mine!

Betty stands dead still as George continues to berate her. ALL SOUND slowly starts to drop out, then comes back abruptly with a RUSH. Suddenly a light snaps on for her and she stares at him.

BETTY
I'm sorry...Oh my gosh, are you George McCord?!

GEORGE
...*What*? What did you call me?

BETTY
George...McCord. You're my favorite actor on...

LYLA
She called you 'George,' George.

BETTY
...did I win some contest?

GEORGE
But I'm David... I mean, I'm not David, but she thinks I am! You heard her...
(looking around the group)
Stop staring at me... I'm not crazy, she is!

BETTY
Why are you screaming at me? I mean, what am I... why am I here? I don't...

GEORGE
You're doing this <u>now</u>? After all the.. are you sick? Are you going to kill me now?

BETTY
No, I... I'll leave. Forgive me if I caused you all any trouble... I just, I don't know how I...
(to George)
... I'm sorry.

George watches Betty walk off the set. The cast and crew try to pretend this scene didn't happen, except for Lyla, who burns a hole into George's back. Their eyes meet.

GEORGE
What?!

132 OMIT 132

133 INT. TV STUDIOS / RECEPTION AREA - DAY 133

George McCord, wearing sunglasses and still angry, strides into the lobby. Charlie and Wesley stand quickly and take out their badges as he approaches.

GEORGE
What can I do for you, gentlemen?

CHARLIE
How do you do, Mr. McCord. We're trying to locate a deranged fan of yours,... a Ms. Betty...

GEORGE
Deranged. That would be the right word.

Wesley takes out the photo of Betty.

GEORGE (cont'd)
That won't be necessary. She's staying with a Rosa something... Hernandez, Herrera. I know it's an 'H' sound... in Silverlake.

CHARLIE
Thanks so much. You must get bothered by this kind of thing a lot.

GEORGE
More than you know. Is there anything else?

CHARLIE
No, that should be more than--

GEORGE
Good.

George turns to leave.

WESLEY
Actually, there is one more thing.

George stops. Wesley is suddenly shy, hesitant.

WESLEY (cont'd)
It's just... well... I watch the show too, and you being Dr. Ravell and all, I thought you could maybe get Jasmine to come out here.

GEORGE
You thought wrong.

George pulls away. Wesley grabs his sleeve.

WESLEY
It's just for an autograph. It's not for me...

GEORGE
It never is.

George wrenches free of Wesley's grip and takes off.

Wesley is furious. He catches George in two strides, spins him around and SLAPS him across the face. George's glasses go skittering across the floor. PEOPLE stare.

WESLEY
You need to learn some manners, friend... reach out to your goddamn fan base a little more.

Charlie pulls Wesley away. George is frozen to the spot, humiliated, a pink handprint emerging on his cheek.

WESLEY (cont'd)
... and I saw your movie-of-the-week. It sucked dick!

134 EXT. HOLLYWOOD BLVD. - DAY 134

Betty walks aimlessly along a busy street. She moves without direction, in a daze until a glint of bright light hits her, causing her to turn. She is staring at a black Lincoln sitting in a car lot, sunlight dancing off its chrome. She shudders involuntarily at it. Suddenly, she hears a familiar voice.

DEL (O.S.)
What the hell are _you_ doing here?

It's Del. He's in a pastel version of his usual shirt, slacks, and tie.

DEL (cont'd)
Well, are you gonna answer me? What'd you come here for?

BETTY
I came for love...

DEL
You're not on that soap opera thing again, are you? 'Cause you know what that is?

BETTY
It's people with no lives watching other people's fake lives.

DEL
That's right. So, if you know it, why are you in trouble?

BETTY
I don't know.

DEL
You sure don't. Who do you think you are coming to Hollywood, anyway? You should remember where you came from. And who you *really* are.

Del looks up at the sun for a moment, shading his eye from it.

DEL (cont'd)
I gotta run. Got some serious clients to meet, with *real* potential.
(BEAT)
Goddamn, it's hot!

He wipes the sweat from his brow. Betty looks at his handkerchief and sees that it's soaked in blood. Then back at his face, now obscured by blood pouring down from his head.

She stares, horrified, and in that moment Del becomes... a MAN, staring back at her as he wipes the sweat from his brow.

MAN
Who are you talking to? Are you crazy?

Betty backs away and melts into the flow of PEDESTRIANS.

135 INT. ROSA'S APARTMENT - LATER 135

Rosa comes home from work and tosses her purse and jacket on the chair. No Betty in her room.

ROSA
Bet-ty!? Did the pizza guy show up yet?

She emerges from Rosa's bedroom with toiletries and moves to an open suitcase in her room. She barely acknowledges Rosa.

ROSA (cont'd)
Are you all right?
(no answer)
What happened?
(BEAT)
He dumped you, didn't he? I KNEW IT WHEN I MET HIM!! He's a loser, like the rest of them. Mother-*fucker*!

Rosa now notices Betty packing.

ROSA (cont'd)
What are you doing?

BETTY
I'm going back to... I need to... I don't know.

Rosa tries to stop Betty for a moment to talk. Betty grabs a pile of Rosa's clothes and heads for her room.

BETTY (cont'd)
... this is your sweater, right?

ROSA
Where are you going?

BETTY
I have to leave now.

She tries to put Betty's suitcase away.

ROSA
What? No, I'm not gonna let you just run out of here... You need to talk about what's going on...

BETTY
You think I'm crazy, Rosa, but you don't know the half of it. My husband was, ahh...

ROSA
Your husband?!

BETTY
Yes, I had a husband and he was killed two weeks ago in my kitchen. I was right there...

Rosa stops.

ROSA
Jesus!... What are you saying?

They stare at each other for a beat.

ROSA (cont'd)
What?! That you had something to do with it?

BETTY
I don't know. I'm just starting to remember it now. I don't...

ROSA
Yeah, but your running away isn't going to help you with all this...

BETTY
There was blood *everywhere*, Rosa. I saw it, I think I watched the whole thing happen... Oh my God...

ROSA
Okay, okay, look, ummm... Let's just talk a little first and you'll feel better, I promise.

The doorbell rings.

ROSA (cont'd)
That's our pizza... You can't go yet.

136 EXT. ROSA'S APARTMENT - DAY 136

Charlie watches Betty undress from a nearby fire escape. He stares at the object of his desperate search with relief and some fascination.

Betty's movements are unhurried, mindless. Charlie stares, mesmerized, until she steps into the shower.

137 EXT. ROSA'S APARTMENT - STREET - SAME TIME 137

Wesley gently nudges open the trunk to Betty's LeSabre. The cardboard cut-out of David Ravell pops out at him.

WESLEY
Whoa! What the fuck're you doing here?

He breaks it over his knee and throws it in the gutter, then quickly removes the wing nut holding the spare tire. He removes the tire, then raises the panel on the floor of the trunk as Charlie joins him.

WESLEY (cont'd)
It's all here. It hasn't been touched.

The bottom of the trunk is lined with brown paper-wrapped bricks of cocaine. Charlie stares at it, shaking his head.

WESLEY (cont'd)
You were right. Del wasn't lying.

CHARLIE
Well, you were right about what that bartender said.

Wesley looks at him. He appreciates the compliment.

WESLEY
But *you* were right first. You gotta follow your instincts.

Charlie takes a long look at Wesley and smiles proudly.

CHARLIE
What do your instincts tell you to do now, kid?

WESLEY
Leave. Take this shit back to Detroit and get the rest of our money.

CHARLIE
We could do that. I could be on my way to Florida, and you could go to Thailand and fuck your brains out.

WESLEY
...but that's not what we're gonna do, is it?

CHARLIE
No... if we don't finish this job, how are we gonna look at ourselves in the mirror? This is it for me, Wesley, she's the last one. My instinct says I gotta see this through with her, and if there's one thing I've tried to teach you here--

WESLEY
It's to follow my instincts. And *my* instincts say get the fuck out of Dodge.

CHARLIE
No, I said to follow 'my' instincts. Now, we go up there and conclude our business. Case closed.

Charlie walks off. Wesley closes the trunk up and prepares to follow him.

WESLEY
... oh, that's fucking democratic.

138 INT. ROSA'S APARTMENT / HALLWAY - MOMENTS LATER 138

At the sound of the BUZZER Rosa goes to the door. She looks through the peephole and sees Charlie holding up a badge.

CHARLIE
I'm Detective Jefferson--

ROSA
Oh... Did Betty call you?

Charlie nods. Rosa opens the door, and he enters with Wesley.

ROSA
She's got problems, but she's no killer. I hope you guys can straighten this out...

Charlie and Wesley exchange a puzzled look.

CHARLIE
We'll do what we can. Where is she?

ROSA
Bet-ty!
(to the men)
Please, go easy on her. She's had a really rough day.

Betty appears. She recognizes the men instantly and freezes. Charlie's eyes wander over her... slowly. Wesley notices.

ROSA (cont'd)
These guys are here to help you, Betty.

BETTY
I don't think so.
(BEAT)
Rosa, I didn't kill Del... they did.

Wesley produces a pistol, sitting Rosa forcibly on the sofa and tapes her mouth and hands. Charlie walks over to Betty.

CHARLIE
We meet again.

He moves closer to her... almost whispers. Wesley steps in and quickly tapes her hands. Charlie stops him.

CHARLIE (cont'd)
Not her mouth...
(to Betty)
I've spent many long hours in a car with your face staring back at me. I've seen it painted on the horizon.

WESLEY
(to Charlie)
What's wrong with you?

A KNOCK at the door ruins Charlie's moment.

ROSA
That's our pizza.

Wesley hustles Rosa out of the room.

CHARLIE
Get rid of them. You understand?

Betty nods, scared, and looks through the peephole. She stares with disbelief at ROY OSTREY. He KNOCKS again. She opens the door a crack.

ROY
Betty! Boy, am I glad to see you!

BETTY
Roy! What are you doing here?

ROY
You're in *serious* danger!

BETTY
Ahh, look, right now's not very...

ROY
I woulda' been here sooner, but Ballard put me in jail. He still thinks you had Del scalped.

BALLARD
I never said that! Open the door, Betty.

BALLARD shoves Roy aside; Charlie's getting edgy ...

BETTY
Sheriff, I don't...

BALLARD
C'mon, Betty, open up! I got some questions for you about...

ROY
Have you checked the trunk of that car you're driving, Betty? I think there might be...

BETTY
It's not really a good time, guys...

BALLARD
Don't give me that. I've come two thousand miles for this!

Charlie has been listening quietly on the other side of the door and finally snaps.

CHARLIE
Two thousand miles? That's nothing!

He flings the door open, sticks a pistol in Ballard's face and yanks them both inside.

CHARLIE (cont'd)
Hah! You probably *flew*! I've crossed the river Styx looking for her, pal! I travelled the fucking country to be here!

Charlie slams the door and frisks them, taking a gun and handcuffs from Ballard. Wesley returns with Rosa.

CHARLIE (cont'd)
(to Betty)
Who are these idiots?

BETTY
This is Roy Ostrey, he's a reporter. And this is Sheriff Ballard. We all went to Fair Oaks High together...

CHARLIE
Oh, this is wonderful...

Wesley takes over. He sits Rosa down on the sofa, then pushes Betty down next to her and beckons to Roy.

WESLEY
Come here.

He breaks Roy's nose with his pistol. Roy crumples to the floor, holding his face. Betty starts to scream, but Charlie puts his hand over her mouth.

Wesley tapes Roy's hands together, then beckons to Ballard.

WESLEY (cont'd)
Your turn.

Ballard drops to his knees in a prayer-like position near the aquarium.

BALLARD
I got two kids and a dog...

Wesley grabs his shirtfront and slams him to the floor, then with a foot on his neck, he loops Ballard's arms around one leg of the steel aquarium stand and handcuffs him.

Charlie does nothing but stare at Betty, his eyes locked with hers. Wesley sees it.

WESLEY
Act professional, remember?

Charlie pulls her to her feet.

WESLEY (cont'd)
What are you doing?

Charlie leads Betty out of the room.

WESLEY (cont'd)
No way! This is *not* professional!

139 INT. BEDROOM - SAME TIME 139

Silence. Then Charlie takes out a knife and cuts the tape from Betty's wrists, touching her hair. Gently. He leaves her standing in the corner while he sits on the edge of the bed.

BETTY
... I s'pose you did that so I could take my sweater off or something.

CHARLIE
No, just stand there... lemme look at you a minute.

She does. Charlie stares intently at her.

CHARLIE (cont'd)
Do you know who I am?

BETTY
... I... I know what you are.

CHARLIE
Do you know why I'm here?

BETTY
I've got a pretty good idea. You're here to kill me, so kill me. You want me to be afraid, but I'm not. I don't care who you are, or why you two killed my husband...

Charlie studies her, then sets his gun down on the bed.

CHARLIE
You really... didn't have anything to do with what Del was doing, did you?

BETTY
I have no idea what he was mixed up in...
it was always something.

CHARLIE
So you weren't involved with him in his
pathetic attempt to diversify?
(off her blank look)
Were you mixed up in the drugs, Betty?

BETTY
Drugs? God, no! I'm totally against
drugs.

CHARLIE
Damn, life is strange. I had you figured
for this cold-blooded, calculating bitch--
Not that I didn't admire you for it.

Charlie slowly folds his knife and pockets it.

BETTY
... well, if you're not going to slit my
throat, why'd you come up here?

CHARLIE
... to see you.

140 INT. ROSA'S APARTMENT - LIVING ROOM - SAME TIME 140

Wesley stands over Ballard, about to tape his mouth. Rosa and Roy are sitting in chairs opposite them, their mouths and wrists already taped.

BALLARD
You killed that bartender in Arizona and
the trucker in Texas, didn't you?

WESLEY
How did you find Betty?

BALLARD
I just put it all together. I knew David,
Lonnie and Chloe were from that show.

Roy starts freaking out, trying to talk through the tape.

BALLARD (cont'd)
Betty thinks they're real people. It
sounded crazy, but it was worth a shot.

Roy is apoplectic...

WESLEY
What do you want?!

Wesley tears his tape off.

ROY
That's a lie! *I* figured it out! I've been trying to tell this dumbass--

BALLARD
Fuck you, Roy Ostrey!

ROY
--small-time, pissant, Barney Fife--

WESLEY
SHUT UP! Shut the fuck up, both of you, before I kill you!

ROY
I'm the one who watched the show...I was...

WESLEY
Did Chloe crack?

ROY
Totally. She came apart like a house of cards. They dropped the charges...

WESLEY
Goddamn... how 'bout Jasmine?

ROY
She's a lesbian.

Wesley immediately pulls his gun and points it at Roy's head.

WESLEY
You lie, motherfucker...

ROY
I swear to God!

Rosa STAMPS her feet, drawing Wesley's attention. She tries to talk through the duct tape; gestures for him to come to her.

WESLEY
What?! You scream, you die.

He yanks the tape off. Rosa winces.

ROSA
I have a tape of today's show.

141 INT. ROSA'S APARTMENT - BEDROOM - SAME TIME 141

Betty is sitting on the bed. Charlie leans against the wall, facing her. He has trouble starting this.

CHARLIE
... I never meet people like you. I'm a garbageman of the human conditon. I deal with trash, mostly, people willing to trade any part of themselves for a few more minutes of their rotten lives. But you... you're different.

BETTY
I am?

CHARLIE
Sure. You could probably have any thing you wanted... somebody as beautiful and stylish as yourself, and you don't even realize it.

Betty looks curiously over at Charlie.

CHARLIE (cont'd)
I'm appreciably older than you, but my health is good. I take care of myself, and I got some money socked away. You'd never have to work agin, that's for sure. I'd treat you like a queen.

BETTY
Umm, I don't think that...

CHARLIE
Wait. Let me get this out.
(clears his throat)
I like the symphony, walks in the rain, sunsets, animals and children. I read passionately, and I like to discuss things. I'm basically conservative, but flexible. I've been involved in the death of thirty-two people, but I can live with that because the world is lighter by thirty-two pieces of shit, excuse my language.

BETTY
"Thirty-two?"

CHARLIE
Well, thirty-three, but I'm not counting Del, on account of you... so, what do you think?
(MORE)

CHARLIE (cont'd)
(BEAT)
You probably feel I'm flattering myself to see us together.

BETTY
I don't feel that, no. I just....I'm not really who you think I am.

CHARLIE
No one is, honey. Here, listen to this... "If who I am and who I hope to be should meet one day, I know they will be friends." Now that's beautiful.

Betty is stunned.

BETTY
I wrote that when I was twelve... where'd you get that?!

CHARLIE
(he pulls out the diary)
I know. I borrowed it from your grandparents because I... I... it doesn't matter. Don't worry, they're fine...
(he gives the diary back)
Look, I used to feel that same way, said practically those same words, sitting at night in a foxhole in Korea...
(BEAT)
I've chased you across the country, Betty, and I come to find out we're a lot more alike than you'd think.

BETTY
I thought you were a garbageman of humanity, or something.

CHARLIE
Yes, but I'd sort of like to put that behind me now...

142 INT. ROSA'S APARTMENT - LIVING ROOM - SAME TIME 142

Wesley is engrossed in watching "A Reason to Love." Behind him, Ballard quietly walks his feet up the wall until he's completely upside down. He rubs one foot against the other until one pantleg is above his cowboy boot. Rosa and Roy watch.

He finally lifts the boot off. It falls soundlessly onto his chest. A small pistol is revealed, holstered above his ankle.

He works the holster open using the edge of the fishtank.

Roy and Rosa COUGH LOUDLY at the same time to cover the noise. Wesley glares at them.

Ballard gets the pistol free. But it falls into the fishtank. The air goes out of Roy's sails. Ballard has fucked up again.

On screen, Chloe and Jasmine kiss and embrace. Wesley reacts as if he was slapped.

WESLEY
... goddamn!

Wesley immediately runs the sequence back to view it again.

Ballard KICKS the wall of the fishtank with his cowboy boot. Roy and Rosa cover the sound again with COUGHING. Wesley pauses the T.V. and looks around.

WESLEY (cont'd)
What's your problem?

Ballard KICKS at the tank again. But he can't break the glass. Roy can't take it any more. He launches himself at the tank, grabs it by the rim and pulls it down on top of himself. A torrent of water, fish, plants and gravel pours down upon him.

WESLEY (cont'd)
You stupid piece of fuck!

He leaps at Roy and starts kicking him savagely. Rosa throws herself onto Wesley's back, knocking him to the floor. Ballard paws through the muck, scattering fish and gravel everywhere. He spots a glint of metal in the sand.

Wesley struggles out from under Rosa. Just as he gets free, Ballard FIRES, hitting him TWICE into his chest. Wesley stares in disbelief at the blood rushing out of him. Then at Ballard, as if trying to link the two.

He slumps to the floor and opens his mouth to scream ...

WESLEY (cont'd)
D-A-A-A-D-D-D-Y-Y-!!!!

Charlie opens the bedroom door.

CHARLIE
Wesley??!

Charlie sees Wesley turn to him as Ballard FIRES again. Wesley's face explodes. The flying lead drives Charlie back to the bedroom.

Crawling through the muck, Roy notices a fish flopping helplessly on the carpet inches from his face.

ROY
Those're Japanese koi!

ROSA
Yes! How'd you know that?

ROY
You gotta get 'em in water right away!

BALLARD
We're in a shootout, Roy! Shut up about the damn fish!

ROY
YOU shut up!
(to Rosa)
They're beautiful, but get them some water.

He gently hands her the fish, then picks up Wesley's nearby gun. Rosa nods; she's amazed that he knew what it was. She looks at Roy in a slightly different way before crawling away toward the kitchen.

143-144 OMIT (NOW IN 141, 142) 143-144

145 INT. ROSA'S APARTMENT - BEDROOM - SAME TIME 145

Charlie FIRES back from the doorway.

CHARLIE
Oh, Christ, they shot my boy!

Enraged, he empties his pistol at the living room. Ballard and Roy return fire, and Charlie ducks back in.

CHARLIE (cont'd)
(reloading)
How the hell did this happen? I'm in a goddamn shoot-out! Wesley? What the fuck happened out there?!

He opens the door, and a bullet slams into the doorjamb near his head. He ducks back in.

Charlie sags against the wall, looking toward Betty.

CHARLIE (cont'd)
That's my son! My son is dead!

BETTY
I'm sorry.

CHARLIE
You're *sorry*? YOU'RE THE REASON WE'RE HERE!

BETTY
WAIT A SECOND! I AM *NOT* THE REASON YOU'RE HERE! I WAS MINDING MY OWN BUSINESS, LIVING A PERFECTLY BORING LIFE UNTIL *YOU* CAME ALONG!

Charlie fights back his grief.

BETTY (cont'd)
What do you want from me?

Charlie can't handle the moment. He breaks for the door, and BLASTS away. This time he's nicked in the shoulder. He stumbles back, losing his balance. His gun falls and slides right into Betty's hand. Equally surprised they stare at one another.

Charlie slumps over in his defeat as Betty holds a shaky pistol on him.

CHARLIE
Oh shit...

146 INT. ROSA'S APARTMENT - LIVING ROOM - SAME TIME 146

Rosa crawls to a flower vase and dumps a second koi into the water inside. Roy and Ballard crouch behind the open archway, using the hanging beads as protection.

BALLARD
(checks his gun)
We need ammo... Go check his jacket, I'll cover you.

ROY
I'm not going out there! Let's wait for the real police...

BALLARD
You gotta go, we're pinned down!

ROSA
So why can't we just sneak outside? Huh?

BALLARD
Lady, you don't just run away from crime... besides, Betty's in there.

ROY
(checking)
You wanna see if he has more shells, go ahead. I say we wait...

BALLARD
No, no, no... you don't know shit about procedure! You don't send your best...

ROY
I've got the working gun, Elden, me! You *wasted* all your bullets so you crawl out there.

Ballard stares at him in disbelief, then back at the closed bedroom door. Ballard starts off on his belly.

BALLARD
Goddammit...

146A OMIT 146A

147 INT. ROSA'S APARTMENT - BEDROOM - SAME TIME 147

A LONG BEAT passes. POLICE SIRENS wail in the distance. Betty moves close to Charlie to look at his shoulder. He watches her intently.

CHARLIE
If we went out that window right now we'd have a chance...

BETTY
I better go check on them.

CHARLIE
Wait, Betty... you still haven't answered me.

BETTY
This is really awkward...

The SIRENS are coming closer. He waves her off.

CHARLIE
Ahh, it's too late, anyway. It's too late.
(BEAT)
Listen, I could shoot my way out, maybe take one of them with me... If you'd gimme my gun back.

BETTY
I'd rather not...

CHARLIE
Betty, I don't wanna shrivel up alone in some stinking prison. No way. I've got some professional pride. And I don't want anybody else to get the credit for taking me out.

BETTY
...what're you saying?

CHARLIE
When a Roman general knew a battle was lost, he'd throw himself on his sword.

Charlie fumbles in his pocket, then pulls out the photo of Betty with the cardboard David Ravell.

CHARLIE (cont'd)
Did... did you really come here because you love this guy?

BETTY
Yes... Not the actor, though, the doctor. I think.

Charlie's sinks slowly to the floor.

CHARLIE
So *all this*...really was because of that soap opera? My son is dead because you came out here to be with that doctor? A fake doctor?

BETTY
I wouldn't have put it quite that way, but...

CHARLIE
Wesley didn't even want to come up here. He warned me, but I insisted...
(BEAT)
I have to ask you, Betty...are you crazy?

BETTY
I don't think I am.

Charlie remains sitting pensively for a long beat.

CHARLIE
I want you to listen to me, Betty. People don't lie when they're about to die.
(MORE)

CHARLIE (cont'd)
(BEAT)
You don't need that doctor. You don't need that actor. You don't need *any* man. It's not the forties, honey. You don't *need* anybody. You've got yourself... and that's more than most people can say.

Charlie reaches out slowly and takes the gun from Betty. She doesn't fight him. He kisses her hand and steps into the bathroom and closes the door. A single GUNBLAST sends a shiver through Betty.

148 INT. LYLA'S HOUSE - NIGHT 148

TV Newscast

CLOSE SHOT of an ANCHORMAN.

ANCHORMAN
In a story that police say is bizarre, even for Hollywood, a father-son team of killers tracked a Kansas soap opera fan halfway across the country, only to find themselves the victims in a final, bloody confrontation...

The Anchorman continues as the CAMERA PULLS BACK to reveal Lyla and George watching television in a plush living room.

LYLA
This story is beyond belief, which is perfect for us. It's free advertising and it's gonna run for months.

GEORGE
I don't think she can do it. You saw what happened.

LYLA
<u>You</u> fucked it up. Who wouldn't freeze in those circumstances? And I don't care <u>*what*</u> her problems are. She wouldn't be the first one in that cast with problems. We have nothing to lose by making her an offer.

GEORGE
What about me? Don't you wanna know how I feel about it? I'm the one who...

LYLA
Why would I give a shit how you feel. And I got news for you. I loved your 'icy water' idea the other day... I'm toying
(MORE)

LYLA (cont'd)
with the idea of killing David Ravell off in a boating accident.

GEORGE
That's not a bad idea. How many episodes before he comes back?

Lyla shakes her head "no."

GEORGE (cont'd)
Jesus, don't do that! If it gets around that you fired me, I'll never land a pilot.

LYLA
Then do as you're told. Get her back.

149 INT. TIP TOP DINER - DAY 149

George and Betty sit across from one another in a booth. Betty listens patiently. Her former co-workers try to remain busy but can't help gawking.

GEORGE
I'm sorry for what I did. It was inexcusable. I'm sorry for the things I said, and for not respecting you, and for all the stupid things that...

Darlene approaches, puts a piece of paper on the table.

DARLENE
When you have a minute...

GEORGE
Look, I don't really like the whole idea of autographs, and I'm kind of in the middle of...

DARLENE
Don't flatter yourself. It's the check.

She walks off.

GEORGE
Oh. Of course... sorry.

BETTY
(grabbing it up)
My treat. You were saying... something about how stupid you've been?

GEORGE
Right... I was. I was an idiot, plain and simple, and I hope you can find it in your heart to forgive me. How's that?

BETTY
Kinda like you'd been saying it since you got on the plane...

GEORGE
I have... did it sound that bad?

BETTY
Mmm-hmm. Listen, I forgive you, Mr. McCord...

GEORGE
George...

BETTY
... George. I do.
(BEAT)
My best friend once said if you were any handsomer it would be a crime...

GEORGE
Thanks...

BETTY
... it's too bad you're such an asshole. 'S the only thing that Del was ever right about.

George winces... accepts it.

GEORGE
No, that's... okay. Fair enough.
(BEAT)
So, now that we've sort of settled the 'asshole' thing, is there any chance you'll come back to the show? At all?

150 INT. TV DINER - DAY 150

Dr. David Ravell sits with Nurse Betty in a diner, catching a bite to eat before going back on shift. They smile at one another over their meals.

BETTY
... there's always a chance, David.

DAVID
Right. But will there be a tomorrow, and the next day, and the next?

BETTY
(whispering to him)
Doctor, if you were any handsomer it'd be a crime...

DAVID
I guess that means you're free tonight. Of course, it's up to you...

BETTY
No, it's up to us. I love you, David. And I want to see you tomorrow, and the next day, and the next day...
(they kiss)

151 INT. TIP TOP DINER - DAY 151

Darlene, the other waitresses, the cooks and assorted customers gather at the counter to watch Betty on television. Sheriff Ballard beams from a nearby stool.

152 INT. SUE ANN'S HOUSE - DAY 152

The kids are out of control, but Sue Ann's oblivious. She leaps from her chair.

SUE ANN
That's my best friend!

153 INT. ROSA'S APARTMENT - DAY 153

Roy, Rosa, Danny and Sra. Herrera watch Betty lean across the table, take David's face in her hands and move into a romantic kiss.

On the sofa, Rosa takes Roy's hand in hers.

POSTSCRIPT:

Rosa Herrera received 11 phone calls off the business cards Betty handed out. But she fell in love with Roy Ostrey, married him and moved to Kansas.

154 EXT. CAFE SISTINA - ROME - DAY 154

Betty watches the pilgrims on their way to St. Peter's as she sips a cup of coffee. HER WAITER stands nearby with one eye on a TV set that broadcasts "A Reason to Love" in Italian.

BETTY
Could I get some service here, please?

Without looking, the waiter approaches, tops off her cup and moves back to watching the show. Betty smiles knowingly at this, takes a sip and settles back in her seat. Slowly, the world passes by.

POSTSCRIPT:

Betty Sizemore appeared in 63 episodes of "A Reason to Love." She is using her earnings to pay for a nursing degree and is currently on vacation in Europe. <u>The</u> Europe.

FADE OUT:

THE END

Nurse Betty *(Renée Zellweger)* with her birthday present, the cardboard cut-out of her hero, Dr. David Ravell

CHARLIE
Morgan Freeman

NURSE BETTY
Renée Zellweger

WESLEY
Chris Rock

DR. DAVID RAVELL
Greg Kinnear

GEORGE McCORD
Greg Kinnear

LYLA
Allison Janney

Top: Betty *(Renée Zellweger)*, Charlie *(Morgan Freeman)*, and Wesley *(Chris Rock)* watching the soap "A Reason to Love."
Bottom: Sheriff Ballard *(Pruitt Taylor Vince)* and Roy *(Crispin Glover)*, the local reporter at the Tip Top Diner.

Top: The two hitmen Charlie *(Freeman)* and Wesley *(Rock)* having lunch at the Tip Top Diner.
Bottom: "So. . . to a successful transaction." Charlie *(Freeman)*, Wesley *(Rock)*, and Del *(Aaron Eckhart)* toast their deal.

Top: George *(Greg Kinnear)* convinces his producer, Lyla *(Allison Janney)*, to hire Betty for the soap.

Bottom: David/George *(Kinnear)* gives Betty *(Zellweger)* motivation for her acting debut on "A Reason to Love."

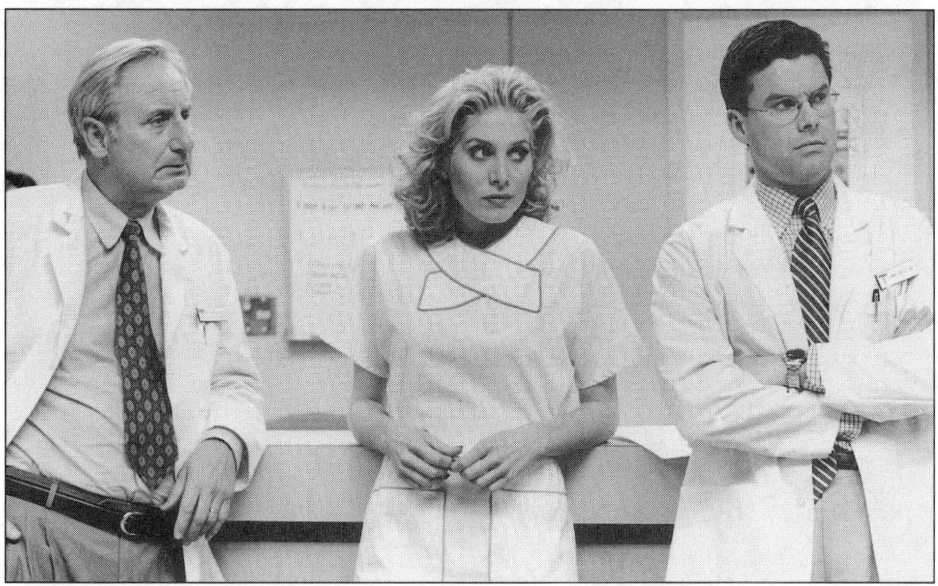

Top: Rosa *(Tia Texada)* befriends Betty when she arrives in Los Angeles.
Bottom: Dr. Lonnie Walsh *(Laird Macintosh)*, Chloe *(Elizabeth Mitchell)*, and Blake *(Steven Gilborn)*, some of the staff at Loma Vista.

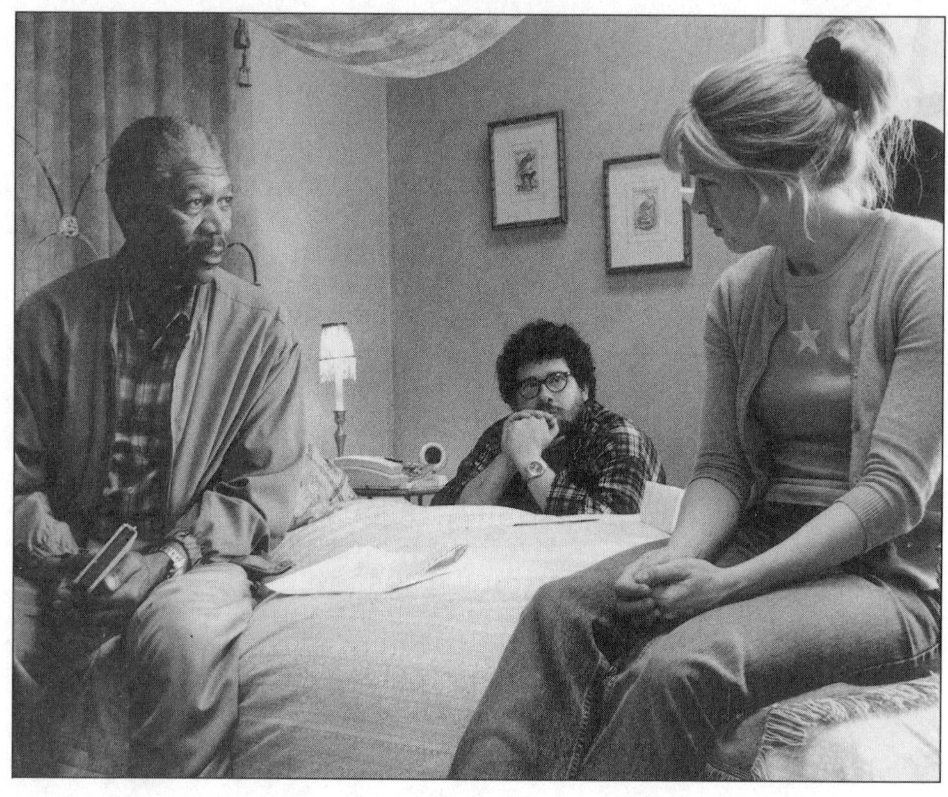

Director Neil LaBute discusses with Renée Zellweger and Morgan Freeman the climactic scene when Charlie finally meets Betty.

CAST AND CREW CREDITS

A Gramercy Pictures presentation in association with Pacifica Film Distribution of a Propaganda Films/ab'-strakt pictures/IMF Production.

Morgan Freeman Renée Zellweger Chris Rock Greg Kinnear

NURSE BETTY

Aaron Eckhart Crispin Glover Pruitt Taylor Vince

Casting by
Heidi Levitt &
Monika Mikkelsen

Music Supervisor,
Frankie Pine

Associate Producers,
W. Mark McNair,
Albert Shapiro

Music by
Rolfe Kent

Costume Designer,
Lynette Meyer

Edited by
Joel Plotch,
Steven Weisberg

Production Designer,
Charles Breen

Director of Photography,
Jean Yves Escoffier

Executive Producers,
Philip Steuer, Stephen
Pevner, Moritz Borman,
Chris Sievernich

Story by
John C. Richards

Screenplay
by John C. Richards &
James Flamberg

Produced by
Gail Mutrux, Steve Golin

Directed by
Neil LaBute

A USA Films Release

CAST

Charlie . . . . Morgan Freeman
Betty . . . . Renée Zellweger
Wesley . . . . Chris Rock
Dr. David Ravell . . . . Greg Kinnear
Del . . . . Aaron Eckhart
Rosa . . . . Tia Texada
Roy . . . . Crispin Glover
Ballard . . . . Pruitt Taylor Vince
Lyla . . . . Allison Janney
Sue Ann . . . . Kathleen Wilhoite
Chloe . . . . Elizabeth Mitchell
Darlene . . . . Susan Barnes
Ellen . . . . Harriet Sansom Harris
Jasmine . . . . Sung Hi Lee
Dr. Lonnie Walsh . . . . Laird Macintosh
Blake . . . . Steven Gilborn
Mercedes . . . . Jenny Gago
Joyce . . . . Sheila Kelley
Merle . . . . Matthew Cowles
Doctor . . . . Wayne Tippit
Grandfather . . . . George D. Wallace
Grandmother . . . . Lesley Woods
Chief Nurse . . . . Cynthia Martells
ER Doctor . . . . Alfonso Freeman
Friend #1 . . . . Kevin Rahm
Friend #2 . . . . Steven Culp
Gloria Walsh . . . . Deborah May
Studio Guard . . . . Michael Murphy
Waitress . . . . Tina Smith
Cook . . . . Mike Kennedy
Rosa's Mother . . . . Irene Olga Lopez
Administrator . . . . Steve Franken
Deputy . . . . Kelwin Hagen
Parking Valet . . . . Joshua Dotson
Woman Patient . . . . Dona Hardy
Grip . . . . Paul Threlkeld
Gang Member . . . . Jose Vasquez
Stagehand . . . . Jack Jacobson
Anchor . . . . Elaine Corral-Kendall
Stunts . . . . Jack Gill, Kevin Scott, Scott Workman, Billy Burton Jr., Tim Gilbert, Kelly Brown, Steve Holaday, Mike Ryan, Mike Cebellos, Simmone Boissereé, Leo Creer Jr.
Directed by . . . . Neil LaBute
Produced by . . . . Gail Mutrux
Steve Golin

Screenplay by . . . . John C. Richards & James Flamberg
Story by. . . . . John C. Richards
Executive Producers. . . . . Philip Steuer
Stephen Pevner
Moritz Borman
Chris Sievernich

THE FILMMAKERS

Director of Photography . . . . Jean Yves Escoffier
Production Designer. . . . . Charles Breen
Edited by . . . . Joel Plotch
Steven Weisberg
Costume Designer. . . . . Lynette Meyer
Music by . . . . Rolfe Kent
Associate Producers. . . . . W. Mark McNair
Albert Shapiro
Music Supervisor . . . . Frankie Pine
Casting by. . . . . Heidi Levitt & Monika Mikkelsen
Unit Production Manager . . . . Tim Clawson
First Assistant Director. . . . . Albert Shapiro
Second Assistant Director . . . . Susan J. Hellmann
Art Director. . . . . Gary Diamond
Set Decorator . . . . Jeffrey Kushon
Location Manager. . . . . John Panzarella
Camera Operator . . . . Michael Chavez
First Assistant Camera . . . . Todd McMullen
Second Assistant Camera . . . . Mike Cassidy
Loader . . . . Robin Bursey
Production Accountant. . . . . Nour Dardari
Post-Production Supervisor. . . . . Steven Kaminsky
Video & Computer Graphics Supervisor . . . . . Elizabeth Radley
Second Second Assistant Director . . . . Philip L. Hardage
Script Supervisor. Alexa Alden
Leadman. . . . . Larry J. White II
Property Master. . . . . Tracy Farrington
Assistant Property Masters . . . . Robert Loyal Good
Nancy M. Bates
Production Coordinator . . . . Karen Ruth Getchell
Graphic Artist . . . . Melissa Mollo
Set Designers. . . . . Henry Alberti
Stan Tropp
Still Photographer . . . . Bruce Birmelin
Sound Mixer . . . . Felipe Borrero, C.A.S.
Boom Operator. . . . . Thomas M. Cunliffe
Cableperson . . . . Anthony Ortiz-Quinones
Special Effects Coordinator . . . . Larz Anderson
Assistant Costume Designer . . . . Kelli Stallings
Costume Supervisor . . . . Shari D. Gray
Costumers. . . . . Mynka Draper
Jennifer Rae Dozier
Key Makeup Artist . . . . Desne Holland
Mr. Freeman's Makeup Artist. . . . . Michael A. Hancock
Ms. Zellweger's Makeup Artist . . . . Sharon Ilson
Mr. Rock's Makeup Artist . . . . Lisa Deveaux
Special Effects Makeup . . . . Cannom Creations, Inc.
Key Hairstylist. . . . . André Blaise
Mr. Freeman's Hairstylist . . . . Deena Adair
Ms. Zellweger's Hairstylist. . . . . Colleen Callaghan
Mr. Rock's Hairstylist. . . . . Scott Julion
Stunt Coordinator. . . . . Charlie Brewer
Assistant Location Managers. . . . . Leslie Thorson
Dan Gorman
David Yrueta
Gaffer . . . . Michael Bauman
Best Boy Electric. . . . . Mark Marchetti
Key Grip . . . . Jorge H. Guzman
Best Boy Grip . . . . Scott "Thumper" Wells
Dolly Grip. . . . . Paul Threlkeld
Rigging Gaffer . . . . Martin Bosworth
Rigging Best Boy Electric . . . . David Diamond
Rigging Key Grip . . . . Al Lieberman
Rigging Best Boy Grip. . . . . Oscar Gomez
Construction Coordinator . . . . Dan Turk
Lead Scenic . . . . Paul Minitello
On-Set Dresser. . . . . Rhonda Paynter
Set Dressers. . . . . Heidi Hublou
Fred M. Paulsen
Jimmy Simeone
Werner Hoetzinger
Standby Painter. . . . . Richard Puga
Transportation Coordinator . . . . Antonio M. Molina
Transportation Captain . . . . Richard Mercier
Transportation Co-Captain . . . . Michael Brum
Picture Car Captain . . . . Jerry A. Oliveri
Video Assist . . . . Eric Roberts
Soap Opera Technical Advisor . . . . Shelly Curtis
Assistant Production Coordinator. . . . . Matt DiFranco
Assistant Accountants . . . . Susan L. Giordano
Paul J. Ballon
Associate Editor. . . . . Joseph C. Bond IV
Assistant Editors . . . . Randy Trager
"Ice" Wade Bartlett
Supervising Sound Editor . . . . Richard E. Yawn, M.P.S.E.
Supervising ADR Editor . . . . Becky Sullivan, M.P.S.E.
Sound Design . . . . Lance Brown
Supervising Foley Editor. . . . . Bob Beher
Sound Editors . . . . Steve Mann, M.P.S.E.
Steve Nelson
Robert Troy
Donald L. Warner Jr., M.P.S.E.
Bernard Weiser, M.P.S.E.
Aaron D. Weisblatt
Assistant Sound Editors . . . . Tim Tuchrello
Shawn Egan
Sound Effects Librarian . . . . Bruce Barris
ADR/Foley Mixers . . . . Eric Thompson, C.A.S.
Shawn Kennelly
Foley Artists . . . . Joan Rowe
Sean Rowe
ADR Recordists . . . . Thor Benitez
Chris Staszak
Re-Recording Mixers . . . . Chris David
Lance Brown
Recordist. . . . . Eddie Bydalek

Re-Recording Engineer. . . . . Michael A. Morongell
Music Editor . . . . Nick South
Orchestrator. . . . . Tony Blondal
Orchestra Contracted by . . . . Seattle Music
Conducted by . . . . Bill Stromberg
Recorded & Mixed by. . . . . Tim Boyle
Assistant Engineer. . . . . Tony Flores
Additional Music Editing. . . . . James Flamberg
Tod Holcomb
Mobile Recording Unit . . Le Mobile Remote Recording Studio
Music Score Mixed at . . . . Conway Studios, L.A.
Additional Orchestration . . . . Kerry Wikstrom
Music Preparation . . . . Atumusica
Extras Casting. . . . . Rich King Casting
Casting Assistants. Leah Buono
Brett Greenstein
ADR Voice Casting . . . . Barbara Harris
Assistant to Mr. LaBute . . . . Zachary Gamburg
Assistants to Mr. Golin. . . . . Gina Amoroso
Garrett Brodie
Assistant to Ms. Mutrux. . . . . Julie Carideo
Assistant to Mr. Steuer . . . . Jeff Gross
Assistant to Mr. Freeman . . . . Quentin Pierre
Assistant to Ms. Zellweger. . . . . Ashley Rogers
Assistant to Mr. Rock . . . . Kali Londono
Unit Publicist . . . . Encore International Group
Michael S. Baumohl
Set Production Assistants . . . . Jeff Bilger
Jadi McCurdy
Mary Holliday
Robert E. Kay
Production Assistants . . . . Christopher Vitale
Smriti Mundhra
Elizabeth Gilman
Post-Production Assistant. . . . . Emily Palmer
Caterer. . . . . In Motion Catering
Craft Services. Peter Evangelatos
Georgia Evangelatos
Set Medic . . . . Robert "Sarge" Hepburn
Second Unit Director . . . . Philip Steuer
Second Unit Director of Photography . . . . Dean Lyras

Rome Unit

Production Services . . . . Panorama Films
Marco Valerio Pugini
Ute Leonhardt
Production Manager. . . . . Fabio Massimo Dell'Orco
First Assistant Director . . . . Enrico Mastracchi Manes
Location Manager . . . . Enrico Latella
Film & Digital Opticals . . . . Pacific Title/Mirage
Main Title Sequence Design . . . . Imaginary Forces
Main & End Title Opticals . . . . Custom Film Effects
Video Mastering . . . . Foto-Kem
Video Mastering Colorist . . . . Tom Sartori
Dolby Sound Consultant . . . . Thom "Coach" Ehle
SDDS Consultant. Benjamin Ing
DTS Consultant. . . . . John Keating

Optical Sound Negative . . . . N.T. Audio
Negative Cutter . . . . Mo Henry
Color Timer . . . . Dan Valliere
Color by . . . . Technicolor

SONGS

"WHATEVER WILL BE, WILL BE (QUE SÉRA, SÉRA)"
Written by Jay Livingston and Ray Evans
Performed by Pink Martini
Courtesy of Heinz Records

"SLOWLY"
Written by Otis Blackwell
Performed by Ann-Margret
Courtesy of The RCA Records Label BMG Entertainment

"I WON'T BE HOME NO MORE"
Written by Hank Williams Sr.
Performed by Hank Williams
Courtesy of Mercury Nashville
Under license from Universal Music Special Markets

"LADY SHAVE"
Written by Sigurdur Kjartansson,Daniel Agust Haraldson,
Birgir Thorarinsson,
Performed by Gus Gus
Courtesy of 4AD
By arrangement with Warner Special Products

"JUST A TOUCH OF LOVE"
Written by Mark Adams, Dan Webster,
Mark Hicks, Raymond Turner, Steven Young,
Thomas Locket, and Steve Arrington
Performed by Slave
Courtesy of Atlantic Recording Corp.
By arrangement with Warner Special Products

"LITTLE LOVEY DOVEY"
Written by Wayne Perry and Tommy Smith
Performed by Texas Joe
Courtesy of Zomba Enterprises, Inc.

"DOUBLE CROSS"
Written by Neal Sugarman
Performed by Sugarman 3
Courtesy of Desco Records

"WHATEVER WILL BE, WILL BE
(QUE SÉRA, SÉRA)"
Written by Jay Livingston and Ray Evans
Performed by Jula De Palma
Courtesy of EMI Italiana SpA

"DON'T YOU KNOW"
Written by Bobby Worth
Performed by Della Reese
Courtesy of The RCA Records Label of
BMG Entertainment

"POOR LITTLE FOOL"
Written by Sharon Sheeley
Performed by Ricky Nelson
Courtesy of EMI Records
Under license from EMI-Capitol Music Special Markets

"THE CATTLE CALL"
Written by Tex Owens
Performed by Eddy Arnold
Courtesy of The RCA Records Label of BMG Entertainment

COLD MORNING"
Written and Performed by
Kitty Kat Stew
Courtesy of Zircon Skye Productions

"IF U DON'T WANT NONE"
Written by T. Stevens and
K. Gardner
Performed by Suga T
Courtesy of Jive Records

"THAT LONESOME MOON"
Written by Wayne Perry and Jerry Marcum
Performed by Willow Creek
Courtesy of Zomba Enterprises, Inc.

"SKUNK WALK"
Written by Neal Sugarman
Performed by Sugarman 3
Courtesy of Desco Records

"CUANDO ME QUIERES"
Written by Marty Blasick &Frankie Pine
Performed by Frankie

Wardrobe Provided by . . . . NikeLevi's
Tuxedos Provided by . . . . Valentino
Classic Hardware Provided by . . . . Kary Cantor
Eyeware Provided by . . . . Calvin Klein
Medical Uniforms Provided by . . . . Landau
Camera Cranes & Dollies Provided by . Chapman/Leonard Studio Equipment, Inc.

The Producers Wish To Thank

Michael Kuhn
Stephen Dickstein
Hualapai Tribe
Peach Springs, AZ
Grand Canyon West

Cameras & Lenses Provided by. . . . . Rocky Mountain
Production Equipment Provided by. . . . . Leonetti Co.

Sound Editing by. Soundstorm
Mixed & Re-Recorded at. . . . . Wilshire Stages
Filmed on. . . . . Kodak Film
International Distribution through . . . . . Summit Entertainment

Aspect Ratio: 2:35/1 [Scope]. . . Dolby Quad, in selected theaters

MPAA Rating: "R"Running Time: 112 minutes

A USA Films Release